Jerry Coyne is 46 and lives in Nottingham, where he works as a bricklayer. He feels that his greatest achievement to date is to have won the love of his wife, Elena, a woman of immense patience and understanding. And his greatest hope is that, one day, he'll be able to leave the memories of his childhood behind him.

# Devil's Child

JERRY COYNE

headline

First published in 2012
by HEADLINE PUBLISHING GROUP

1

Cataloguing in Publication Data is available from the British Library

978 0 7553 6269 1

Typeset in Adobe Garamond by Palimpsest Book Production Limited,
Falkirk, Stirlingshire

Printed and bound in Great Britain by CPI Group (UK) Ltd,
Croydon, CR0 4YY

Headline's policy is to use papers that are natural, renewable and recyclable products
and made from wood grown in sustainable forests. The logging and
manufacturing processes are expected to conform to the environmental regulations
of the country of origin.

HEADLINE PUBLISHING GROUP
An Hachette UK Company
338 Euston Road
London NW1 3BH

www.headline.co.uk
www.hachette.co.uk

This book is dedicated to every adult who suffered abuse as a child and to every child who is being abused today. If my story encourages just one person to seek justice, telling it will have been worthwhile.

# *Acknowledgements*

I am very grateful to the people who have made it possible for me to tell my story and who have supported me through the dark days.

My wonderful wife, **Elena**, who is a true angel and a remarkable woman. For the last eight years, she has put a smile on my face and has seen me through my frequent nightmares and flashbacks without complaint. She has given me a reason to live, and when I wake up every morning and see her beautiful smiling face and she tells me that she loves me, I know I am truly blessed. There is nothing more beautiful than the love she surrounds me with.

**Mark Keeley**, my solicitor (at Freeth Cartwright Nottingham), who believed in me and supported me through my court case. He is the best man I have ever met, although he's so unassuming that I'm sure he doesn't have any idea just how great he is.

**Jane Smith**, who believed in my book. I knew within

ten minutes of meeting Jane that she was the right person to help me write it, and I will be eternally grateful to her for all her hard work and determination.

**Steve and Sarah Cockburn**, my best friends. Thank you for just being you. Your friendship is so valuable to me.

Life is what you make it; life is a gift I've learned to enjoy.

# Chapter One

There was a light shining down on me from above. I could see it clearly, even though my eyes were closed. And that's when I realised I must be dead.

I'd once heard two men talking about their near-death experiences – I think it was on one of the TV chat shows I watched sometimes, always with a sense of guilty depression because I didn't have anything better to do in the middle of a weekday afternoon. At the time, I'd been struck by the fact that they both described the same thing: a brilliant, almost-white light they'd felt compelled to move towards. Of course, neither of the men on the TV programme had actually died in the end – something had happened in both cases to prevent them following the light. But it looked as though the outcome for me was going to be different and I wasn't going to get the chance to tell my story on a chat show.

I was surprised by how calm I felt as I lay waiting for

the angels to find my soul and guide me to the gates of heaven. At least, I hoped that was what was going to happen, because the horrible thought had just struck me that perhaps the nuns had been right and I *was* the Devil's child. I had no idea what the standard procedure would be then – although I was pretty certain it wasn't going to be something I wanted to try to imagine – and I just hoped it wasn't too late for God to decide to forgive my mortal sins and snatch me back from the jaws of hell.

I'd been brought up as a Roman Catholic – as you may already have guessed – and although a lot of things had happened to me as a child to make me doubt the existence of God and to turn me against the Church as an institution, part of me still believed what I'd been taught. So I wouldn't have been surprised if angels had appeared to guide me to the Kingdom of Heaven – I just hadn't expected it to happen so early in my life.

I seemed to be lying on my back, and as I moved my head cautiously to one side, I felt a terrible pain, as though someone had grasped me by the throat with fingers of burning steel. I couldn't breathe, and I began to panic. I gasped for air and, as I did so, I raised my hand and touched the raw, lacerated skin on my neck. Which is when the thought struck me: *If I'm dead, I shouldn't be able to feel pain, unless . . .*

I released a single, choking sob and tried to block the

incomplete thought from my mind. But it was too late:
*. . . unless the nuns had been right about me and I was truly*
*condemned to hell, where I would suffer the agonies of eternal*
*damnation.*

The last thing I could remember was shouting at my
girlfriend, Sarah, and feeling as though I wanted to cry. I
remembered, too, the look in her eyes as her anger turned
to something else – distress perhaps, or even fear. I had
no memory of what happened after that, but as my fingers
gently explored what felt like the burned skin on my neck,
I groaned, and a woman's voice said, 'Hello, Jerry. So
you're with us at last. Don't try to sit up.' A hand touched
my shoulder, pushing me firmly but gently back down on
to the bed, and the same voice asked, 'Do you know where
you are?'

I could hear other voices too, although I wasn't sure if
they were real or inside my head. I tried to concentrate,
but the thoughts were all jumbled up, as though they were
solid objects that were moving around in my mind in a
sort of perpetual motion. Until then, I'd kept my eyes
tightly shut, but now I opened them, slowly and cautiously.

I couldn't see much at first – just the light above me
and the blurred outline of a woman's face. But none of
what I *could* see seemed to fit at all with my idea of heaven.
Perhaps the nuns had simply been wrong when they
described it to us – as I'd discovered they were about so

many other things. However, the really good news was that it didn't look much like hell either.

In fact, I wasn't dead – as you've probably also guessed – although apparently it wasn't for want of trying.

I turned my head a fraction of an inch towards the voice and tried to say 'no' in answer to the question about knowing where I was. But instead of speaking, I made a dry, rasping sound and then gasped as a white-hot bolt of pain shot up my neck and into my head.

'It's all right, Jerry,' the voice said, and again a hand touched my shoulder. 'You're safe here. You're in a hospital. The doctor will be in to see you soon. You're lucky to be alive, you know.'

It was a reliable, trustworthy sort of voice, and I decided to believe it and to accept that I *was* alive, although I wasn't so sure about being lucky. To me, good fortune doesn't involve having a raw, searing pain in your neck and throat and feeling as though your brain is about to explode through the top of your skull. I was prepared to take her word for it though – for the time being, at least.

Very cautiously, I turned my head until I could see the dark-haired young woman who was standing beside the bed on which I was lying. Again I tried to speak, to ask what had happened to me, but this time I just made an ugly gurgling noise, and the woman patted my shoulder as she said, 'Don't try to talk, Jerry. The doctor will be here any minute.'

Someone had moved the light above the bed so that it was no longer shining directly down on me, but I closed my eyes as I tried to remember what had happened.

Had I been involved in a car accident? Maybe my seatbelt had become tangled around my neck, bruising my throat and causing the painful lacerations I could feel with the tips of my fingers. Or maybe I'd been mugged, or got into a fight. In fact, that was a more likely explanation, because although I'm normally a pleasant-enough, mild-mannered man, something happens to me when I've had a few drinks and I become more like whichever the bad one was of Dr Jekyll and Mr Hyde. Alcohol makes me argumentative to the point of belligerence, so it wasn't too much of a stretch of the imagination to believe I'd been drinking in a bar somewhere and got into a fight. I just hoped the other bloke was feeling worse than I was.

For some reason, the next thought that struck me was that perhaps I'd been stabbed. I began to touch the bits of my body I could reach, feeling, very tentatively, for a stab wound. But although I clearly had several bruises, the only broken skin – on the upper part of my body, at least – appeared to be on my neck. Even to my befuddled and confused mind, it didn't seem likely that my injuries had been the result of someone trying to strangle me with their bare hands in a bar-room brawl. So perhaps I'd been jumped on my way home and the cuts and painfully burned skin around my neck had been caused by some sort of ligature.

Suddenly, my heart started to thump and my whole body was instantly drenched in sweat. It was the thought of something tied around my neck that did it. I began to panic, and felt as though I was falling backwards off an infinitely high mountain, while darkness rushed up to envelop me.

I knew I had to get up and get out of the hospital. I dug my elbows into the mattress, using all my strength to try to raise my head and shoulders off the bed and look around me. The woman with the kind face had gone and although the room was full of people, no one seemed to be looking in my direction. So I lowered my legs over the side of the bed and sat there for a moment, trying to reassure myself with the thought that if I was really badly hurt, the doctor would have come by now.

There were people lying on beds and trolleys, their faces pale and pinched with pain, and others sitting in chairs, dishevelled and bemused, while tired-looking nurses cleaned and stitched their wounds and tried not to inhale the rancid stench of alcohol.

The smell of hospitals has always made me feel faint and nauseous, and as I bent down to look under the bed for my trainers, I thought I was going to pass out. I sat up again quickly and waited for the feeling to fade before calling out to a nurse who was bustling by, 'I can't find my shoes. They're not under the bed. Where will they have put my shoes?'

The nurse stopped and looked at me with a quizzical expression, as though she was trying to distinguish my face from the many others she'd seen and barely had time to register that night. Then she shrugged as she said, 'You didn't have any shoes when you were brought in,' and hurried away.

*That's odd*, I thought. *What sort of accident or fight would have involved the removal of my shoes? Sarah will be cross with me when I arrive home in just my socks.*

For some reason, the thought of Sarah made me feel sad. In my mind, I could hear the sound of raised voices and doors slamming, and then I felt the surge of anxiety I always feel when I know I've done something wrong.

Had Sarah and I had a fight? It seemed likely, if only because we had quite a lot of rows in those days. But I couldn't imagine Sarah ever doing anything to hurt me, however angry she might be with me. In fact, most of our arguments were my fault. I was the one who usually went off the deep end – often for reasons I couldn't explain, even to myself. So had I done it again? Had I manufactured a quarrel with Sarah because I needed an outlet for the fear and self-disgust that regularly built up inside me until it felt like a huge wave that was going to drown me? I hated my anger, but sometimes I didn't seem to be able to stop it erupting out of me – although the booze didn't help, of course.

I walked quickly along the pavement, away from the hospital, still thinking about Sarah and how I was killing our relationship because I couldn't put into words – to her or to anyone else – what was really wrong with me. And then, just as I rounded the corner at the end of the road, a police car pulled up beside me and two policemen jumped out of it.

'Left in such a hurry we forgot to put on our shoes, did we, sir?' one of the policemen asked me, in a tone of mock politeness.

'What's it to you?' I snapped back at him. 'Walking in your socks isn't a crime as far as I'm aware.'

'You're right,' the second policeman said. He was standing directly in front of me, his legs slightly apart and his hands on his hips. 'But threatening your girlfriend *is*. The girlfriend's had enough, mate. She's applying for a restraining order against you. So the good news is that you'll be able to manage without your shoes tonight, because we're going to give you a lift. Of course, where there's good news, there's always bad: I'm arresting you, and the lift we'll be giving you will be to the police station.'

Later, the duty sergeant asked me what I could remember about the events of that day, before I'd woken up in hospital. 'Nothing,' I told him. 'Although if I got into a fight, I think I must have lost, because every inch of my body aches and I feel as though I've had a bloody good kicking.'

'No, it wasn't a fight,' the sergeant told me. 'You tried to hang yourself. Apparently, you'd stopped breathing by the time a couple of your neighbours cut you down. You're very lucky to be alive.'

Lucky. It was what the nurse had said at the hospital. But if I was so bloody lucky, why did I feel empty and miserable?

I stepped into the bleak, narrow cell and heard the door slam shut behind me. There was a window at the end of the room, made up of lots of small panes of thick, opaque glass that let in some light but stopped you being able to see out. And underneath the window was a concrete bed, on top of which was a thin, blue, neatly folded plastic mattress. I spread the mattress out and sat down, resting my elbows on my thighs and putting my head in my hands as I tried to remember what had happened earlier that day.

If I was honest, I knew my relationship with Sarah was at rock bottom – it had been for some time – and that its slow and painful demise was probably mostly my fault.

I'd done what I always did with anything good in my life – systematically tested it and put it under so much pressure and strain that it eventually shattered into a million pieces. So if Sarah *had* filed for a restraining order – as the policeman said – it meant that, once again, I'd succeeded in destroying something that really mattered to me.

I went to court the next morning, and was ordered to stay away from Sarah. Apparently, not long after we'd had a particularly distressing argument, I'd fixed a piece of wood across the hatch into the loft of the house we shared, stood on a chair while I tied one end of a set of jump leads around the wood and the other end around my neck, and then kicked the chair away. Sarah thought I was dead, and I was certainly unconscious by the time she'd run to a neighbour's house and they'd managed to cut me down.

The only thing I could remember about that day, though, was waking up in the morning with such a deep sense of despair and hopelessness that I simply didn't know how I was ever going to get past it and move on with my life.

I'd attempted to kill myself before – several times, in fact, the first being when I was just a little boy. But I don't think I'd really wanted to die. I'd just wanted the nightmares and the flashbacks and the relentless unhappiness of every minute of every day to stop. That day, though, when I realised how close I'd come to succeeding, I knew I had to find some way of accepting what had happened to me when I was a child and take control of my life – although, of course, as with so many things, that was easier said than done.

I didn't blame Sarah for finally saying 'enough'. For a long time, I'd been using alcohol to try to blot out the pain of my memories and loosen the tentacles of depression that had wrapped themselves around my mind and were squeezing all the hope out of me. I often didn't sleep at night, and in the mornings I barely had enough energy to drag myself out of bed. So I'd stopped functioning normally, and then I'd stopped going to work.

Sarah had tried her best to help me. In fact, she'd been sympathetic and put up with my moods for longer than anyone could reasonably have been expected to. Gradually though, my nightmares had become her nightmares, and when I'd started turning my anger on her, she finally decided – quite rightly – that she couldn't take it anymore.

One morning, a few days after I'd tried to hang myself and Sarah had kicked me out of the house, I woke up with a single thought echoing loudly in my head: I knew it was time to face my fear and take some sort of action to try to sort out my life.

An hour later, I was on the bus heading for Nottingham city centre, where I walked through the front door of the offices of Freeth Cartwright Solicitors and stood nervously in the reception area.

There were three girls at the reception desk, and for a moment I just stood there, looking at them. I knew it would only take one brusque or unkind word to make me turn tail and run back out through the door. So, while the girls watched me – at first with polite anticipation and then with slightly uncomfortable expressions on their faces – I tried to decide which of the three of them was likely to be the most sympathetic. Eventually, I took a deep breath, looked directly at the fair-haired girl, who smiled at me with patient encouragement, and said, 'I . . . I wanted . . . I thought . . . W . . . W . . . Would it be . . .? Can I speak to someone?'

My stammer was so bad I was surprised when she seemed to understand what I'd said and told me, 'I'm afraid there's no one available today. But I can make an appointment for you to see someone later in the week.'

'No!' I almost shouted the word and then felt myself blush with embarrassment. 'I'm sorry,' I said, more quietly. 'It's just . . . It's really, really important. I have to see someone today. Please.'

I was still stammering painfully and, after a moment, the girl nodded her head and smiled again as she said, 'All right.' Then she pointed towards some expensive-looking chairs that were arranged around a low glass table and added, 'Take a seat and I'll see what I can do.'

As I sat in the waiting area, biting the skin at the side of my thumb, I focused my attention on the mahogany-cased clock on the wall opposite me and tried to suppress my desire to run. It was a warm day, but it wasn't the temperature that was making me sweat so profusely. I was twenty-eight and I'd never told my story to anyone. So why had I thought it would be a good idea to tell it to a total stranger?

I suddenly felt sick. I couldn't do it. It had been a stupid idea. I stood up, and at that moment a tall, dark-haired man in a well-cut suit walked towards me and held out his hand.

'Mr Coyne?' His tone was businesslike, but he seemed friendly enough as he shook my damp, sweating hand. 'I'm Julian Middleton. Why don't we go somewhere we can talk?'

I nodded and followed him silently down a long corridor and into a large, high-ceilinged room, where he pulled out a chair from under the largest table I had ever seen in my life and said, 'Please, sit down.' Then he sat down beside me and asked, 'Now, how can we help you?'

My mouth was dry and I had to swallow several times before taking a deep breath and blurting out, 'I was sexually abused as a child. I have flashbacks and nightmares and I've just tried to hang myself. But I don't really want to die. I just want to be able to live a normal life. And I need help.'

Tears were streaming down my face and my stammer was worse than it had ever been as I talked for the first time about what had happened to me. It felt as though I'd put my fingers inside my chest and ripped it open, exposing the deepest, most private parts of my being to this stranger I couldn't even look in the eyes. I'd taken a huge step – a step I hadn't believed I would ever take – and I knew there was no going back, because it was probably my one chance of having a future. It was a heavy burden to place on someone else's shoulders, but all I could do was hope and pray that Julian Middleton would accept at least temporary responsibility for the story of my life and try to find some way of helping me.

It was a difficult story for anyone to hear, and although I only told a very small part of it to Julian Middleton that day, he often looked away, out of the window, while I was talking. Then, as I stuttered and stammered to a halt, there was silence for a moment and I could feel myself flushing red with humiliation and with the distress of knowing he probably thought I was crazy.

I imagined he was trying to think of the best way to get me out of the building with the minimum amount of fuss. So I was amazed when he cleared his throat and said, in a quiet, respectful voice, 'Well, Mr Coyne, I do think we might be able to help you. I'm going to make an appointment for you to see my colleague, Mark Keeley.

He's the best man for this job, I think.' And then he looked me directly in the eyes as he added, 'Of course, if that's all right with you?'

I didn't sleep that night, and the next day, when I returned to the offices of Freeth Cartwright Solicitors, I met Mark Keeley. At first sight, I wasn't sure whether he really was the right man for this particular job. In his pinstriped suit, shoes so shiny you could almost see your face in them, and oval, wire-rimmed glasses, he looked far too young and wet behind the ears to be a real, fully fledged solicitor. How wrong I was! Fifteen years later, he's still my solicitor, as well as being the man I admire more than any other I've ever met. He guided me through some terrible times, when I didn't think I was going to be able to carry on. More importantly though, he listened to everything I told him with patience and compassion, and he believed me. He's the rock that underpins my sanity, although I'm sure that, even now, he has no real understanding of what he did for me that day and all the days that followed it.

I still have nightmares and flashbacks about what happened to me when I was a child, and there are times when I can't shake off the crushing weight of self-loathing. But I've accepted that the pain is never going to go away completely, and I'm determined to be strong and not allow it to overwhelm me.

Jerry Coyne

Although I'm not a bitter man, there are people I will never forgive for what they did to me, people who – despite my desire to be a 'good' person – I ardently hope will rot in hell and never see the white light of salvation or hear the beating of angels' wings when the time comes for their stained and blackened souls to leave their mortal bodies.

I know that seems a terrible thing to say, but perhaps you'll understand why I feel that way when you've read the story of my childhood.

# Chapter Two

Both my parents were Irish immigrants who met and married in Nottingham. In fact, my dad was almost a caricature of the sort of 'archetypal Irishman' who gives some of his compatriots a bad name. He worked as a labourer on building sites, and when he wasn't at work, he was drinking with his mates, while my mother stayed at home to look after the children – six of us when I was born – and to do service as a punch bag for him when he got back from the pub at night.

My mother must have grown weary of all the cuts and bruises and of living without love, because when I was just a few weeks old, she walked out of the house one day while my dad was at work, locked the front door behind her and ran off to London, leaving us kids home alone.

Becoming a single parent within the space of just one working day must have been more than a bit of a shock for our dad, who'd never really been any kind of parent at all and to whom we were nothing but a damned nuisance. The neighbours helped out as much as they could, mostly by leaving pans of food on the front doorstep while Dad was out at the pub, and my oldest sister, Geraldine – who was seven when I was born – cooked, cleaned, changed nappies and did her best to take care of my two other sisters, my brother and me.

I had another brother, too, who was nine when our mother left and who suffered from multiple sclerosis and unspecified mental problems and had already been taken away to live in an institution. And it wasn't long before Dad decided to get rid of the rest of us as well. I expect we were cramping his style. Or perhaps what really pissed him off was the fact that he had to spend money on feeding us which he'd rather have spent on even more alcohol. It doesn't matter now what his reasons were. The upshot was that we were taken into care when I was three months old and sent to live with all the other abandoned children and orphans at Nazareth House in Nottingham.

Nazareth House was a home in two parts – one for old people and the other for children like us. It was run by Catholic nuns of the order of the Poor Sisters of Nazareth and was a grand place to live. Mealtimes were regular and – once I'd graduated from bottled milk – the food was plentiful and good. I was with my brother and sisters, I had a warm cot to sleep in, clean clothes to wear and lots of other children to play with me and fuss over me. So, for the next four years, I was like the proverbial pig in clover.

My earliest memory is of standing up in my cot in a room like a hospital ward that had other cots and beds lined up along two of the walls. I was a popular baby and I never had to wait long before a member of staff or a child picked me up. I don't remember having a lot of contact with my brother John – who was liked by everyone and who, as I got older, became my idol and my hero – but I did get plenty of attention from my sisters. Every morning, before they went to school, Geraldine, Teresa and Carmella would lift me out of my cot and cuddle me, telling me what a fine boy I was and that I must be sure to be good all day. Then, when they got back to the home after school, they'd kiss me and play with me and laugh when I wrapped my chubby toddler's arms around their necks and tried to say their names.

For four years I felt secure and safe. If I'd ever thought about it at all – which, as a young child, I don't think I did – I'd have assumed that all children lived like we did, in large houses with lots of other children, looked after by nuns. I had no memory of living with my mum and dad – in fact, my sister Geraldine was the only 'mum' I'd ever known – so I didn't miss them. I'm pretty sure I was happy, because although I only have snatches of memories of those first four years, all of them involve good things, like being hugged, kissed and played with.

Then a new nun arrived at the children's home and everything changed.

My first complete memory of that time is of being slapped across the face and of tumbling head over heels down some stairs while a nun I didn't know shouted at me, 'You're the Devil's child.' I'd never heard of the Devil before then, but I knew by the tone of her voice that being his child wasn't something good.

I landed at the bottom of the stairs and lay there for a moment, dazed by shock and with pain in every part of my body. The nun had run down the stairs after me and I cried out as she grabbed a handful of my hair and dragged me to my feet, pulling me down another flight of stairs to the playroom and chanting, in an angry, eerily singsong voice, 'Devil's child, Devil's child.'

Until that day, someone had always come when I cried, to wipe away my tears and ask, in a gentle, cooing voice, 'What's wrong, Jerry? Don't cry now, pet.' This time, though, no one dried my tears when I sobbed, and I remember feeling confused when the nun tugged harder at my hair and then lashed out with her foot, kicking me in the back so that I shrieked with pain.

I was too stunned to struggle or try to resist as she dragged me into the corner of the playroom and hissed,

'Put your hands on your head and face the wall, Devil's child.' So I stood there, staring at the wall through a haze of tears, not understanding what had just happened.

The playroom had been empty when we entered it, and when I finally stopped sobbing, it was silent. Thinking that the nun must have gone, I lowered my hands from my head and turned around. She was standing with her hands on her hips and a humourless smile on her face. Her arm shot out towards me like the forked tongue of a snake, and she spun my head round so that I was facing the wall again. Then, grasping hold of the hair on the back of my head and twisting her fingers into it until I cried out in pain, she smashed my face against the wall again and again, until I fell in a heap on the floor at her feet.

I lay there for a moment, with my hands covering my head, feeling dizzy and sick and making a small whimpering sound like a frightened animal. And when I finally found the courage to look up from under my arm, the nun had gone.

I didn't tell anyone what had happened. I don't know why. Perhaps it was partly because I couldn't make any sense of it myself and felt I must have done something very bad for someone to treat me that way. I suppose, too, that I was trying to work out the reason why the new nun had clearly taken such an instant and profound dislike to me.

After that day, Sister Dominic often gave me sneaky slaps when no one was looking, and I soon learned to keep out of her way and to hide whenever I saw her coming. Unfortunately, though, she didn't have the same desire simply to avoid me. Instead, she seemed determined to disseminate the powerful hatred and spite she felt towards me by telling lies about me to the other nuns and eventually convincing them that I was bad and that it was their Christian duty to beat the wickedness out of me.

Before long, even the nuns and members of staff who had been the kindest and most loving towards me seemed to have turned against me, and I often suffered harsh and brutal punishments, which were made even more difficult to accept by the fact that I'd never before been punished in any way for anything.

It was as though everyone had started speaking a completely different language I didn't understand. Almost overnight, the world I had always felt safe in had disappeared and had been replaced by one that was governed by rules no one had explained to me and I couldn't work out for myself.

If I close my eyes, I can still see clearly the hate-filled face of the nun who changed my life when I was four years old. From that point on, I seemed to be blamed for everything and I was always getting into trouble without understanding why. Often, while the nuns were on their knees in the chapel, praying and asking God to forgive their sins, I'd be put to work scrubbing the floor. And if they weren't satisfied with what I'd done – which they almost never were – they'd make me do it again, until my knees were aching, my hands were red and sore and I was weeping with tiredness and miserable frustration.

One night, something woke me up and my heart was already racing when I opened my eyes and saw the outlines of three black figures standing beside my bed. I cried out, and immediately a hand was clamped over my mouth and nose. Instinctively, I started kicking my legs and thrashing around in my bed, panicking and trying to loosen the grip of the hand so that I could breathe again. Then a voice hissed angrily in my ear, 'Keep still. Stop struggling. Be quiet and do as I say.' So I lay perfectly still and looked up into the face of the nun who hated me.

Behind her, a shaft of light was shining into the dark room through the open doorway, and for a moment it looked as though it was coming from her head. I gasped in fear, and the hand once again clamped down on my mouth as I was lifted out of my bed. I thought, fleetingly, about sinking my teeth into the rough palm of the hand and shouting to wake up the other children, who were still sleeping peacefully in their beds. But before I even had a chance to try to open my mouth, I had been whisked out of the room.

There were two other nuns with Sister Dominic. One of them held me by the ankles and the other by the wrists as they bumped and bundled me down the corridor, away from the bedrooms and into a room in another part of the building. It was a dingy room, bare except for a metal-framed bed covered with a grey woollen blanket and a huge crucifix hanging on one of its walls.

I was lifted up until my face was almost touching the cross and then Sister Dominic slapped my head and said, 'Say "I am the Devil's child".'

I whimpered and twisted my body in an attempt to loosen the painful grip on my arms, and she slapped me again, hissing at me, with her mouth so close to my ear I could feel the heat of her angry breath, 'Say it.'

'I am the Devil's child,' I whispered.

'Louder!' Sister Dominic struck my back with her clenched fist. 'Say it louder.'

'I am the Devil's child,' I said again. I didn't understand what the words meant, but as the tears rolled down my cheeks, I was filled with fear because, somehow, I knew I'd just made a terrible confession.

The next minute, I seemed to be flying through the air, and as I crashed, face down, on to the bed, Sister Dominic began to tear my pyjamas off my shivering body. I was still lying on my stomach when the nuns tied my hands to the rail at the head of the bed, bound my feet together and began to pray. As they murmured and chanted their prayers, they threw holy water on to my naked body, and each icy-cold drop made me wince, so that I twisted my wrists and the ties around them tightened and chafed my skin.

When they loosened the bindings around my wrists and turned me over on to my back, I tried to sit up. But Sister Dominic pushed me back down, re-tied my hands and started to punch me repeatedly in the groin, saying as she did so, 'You are the Devil's child. The Devil has taken possession of your body and he must be beaten out of you.'

The other nuns started to hit me too, and when the intensity of the pain became greater than that of my fear of what they'd do to me if I made a noise and someone heard me, I screamed. Immediately, one of the nuns pushed a piece of material into my mouth and I retched and then began to flail around on the bed, terrified that I was going to swallow the material and choke to death. And as I gagged and panicked, the nuns continued to hit me, slapping and punching my body until I was hysterical and barely able to breathe.

Then the beating stopped abruptly and Sister Dominic undid the ties around my wrists before pulling me up off the bed by my arms.

'Kneel!' she barked at me. 'Kneel down before the

crucifix, Devil's child, and pray to God to save your blackened soul.'

I was four years old and I was frightened – almost literally out of my wits. Although I was a lively, occasionally unintentionally cheeky little boy, I'd never knowingly done anything bad in my short life. So what could possibly have blackened my soul? And what sort of God would sanction such vicious and brutal abuse of anyone, let alone of a child? But I was too young to rationalise what I was being told, so I knelt on the cold, bare floor of that cell and prayed with all my heart that God would drive the Devil out of me and make me good.

After what seemed like hours, the nuns carried me back to my room, dropped me on my bed, untied the material that still bound my ankles together, threw my pyjamas on top of me and told me that if I ever breathed a word to anyone about what had happened, something far more terrible would be done to me.

After they'd gone, I lay in bed in a state of shock and sobbed silently into my pillow. I hated myself for having done something so bad that it warranted such cruel punishment and for being so stupid that I didn't even realise what it was I'd done. And then, eventually, traumatised and exhausted, I fell into a fitful, nightmare-filled sleep.

I lay awake for a long time every night after that. I didn't know how the Devil had got inside me, but I did know that I couldn't risk it happening again. So I lay on my back, crossed my arms over my chest and prayed fervently to God to protect me from evil. I was terrified of falling asleep, because I was convinced that as soon as I shut my eyes, the Devil would come back to get me – and then the nuns would have to try to beat him out of me again.

I have no memory of ever being frightened before that time. Of course, I'd had the same anxious moments that all young children have – when they hurt themselves, or are startled by something, or wake up alone in the night. But now I was frightened of everything – including and particularly the dark, the Devil, and the nuns, with their black robes and cowls and their cold, angry faces.

Nuns came back to my room on other nights after the first one, and despite my determination never to let down my guard and fall asleep, I'd wake up with a start to find them standing around my bed like a coven of witches. Sometimes they'd be chanting in low, murmured voices – 'Devil's child, Devil's child' – and sometimes they'd hit me, with their bare hands, or with wooden coat hangers, or slippers.

Even on the nights when they didn't come, I'd often wake up and, with my heart thumping, strain to hear what I imagined were their whispered voices outside the bedroom door. And then, one night, I hit on the idea of sleeping under my bed so that when they did come, they wouldn't be able to find me.

Although it was cold, lying on the bare floor in my pyjamas, I felt safer there than in my bed, and the discomfort helped to keep me awake – and as long as I was awake, the Devil couldn't get me. But on the third night the nuns came in, dragged me out from my hiding place and beat me again, this time for not being in my bed.

After that, I started sleeping at the bottom of the bed, curled up into a foetal ball under the blankets. It was hot and I was barely able to breathe, but I felt less vulnerable than I did with my head on the pillow, where I was easy prey for both the Devil and the nuns.

By the time I started primary school, I knew enough about the religion I was being brought up in to be aware that the Devil was always watching us, waiting for us to fall from grace and commit a sin, so that he could snatch us up and take us away to suffer with him in hell. Although I was too young really to understand what I was being told, I already had some idea of what was involved in trying to drive the Devil out of someone he'd got into. So it was dread at the thought of him getting inside me again that made me pray so eagerly before every meal and then again on my knees in front of the statue of the Virgin Mary before I went to bed each night.

It seemed that with every month that passed, the nuns'

attacks on me became more vicious and determined. Perhaps it was because I was trying to hide my hurt and confusion beneath an outward show of bravado by answering back cheekily whenever I was ticked off or told to do something, whereas what I really wanted to do was burst into tears and shout at everyone, 'Why don't you like me anymore?'

I was five when I was enrolled at St Patrick's Primary School, and for the first few months I loved it. The teachers were kind and patient and made everything fun, and being at school for a few hours every day was a welcome relief from my life at Nazareth House. But because of my night-time punishments and my fear of falling asleep, I was finding it increasingly difficult to concentrate. I'd often sit in the classroom at school, hearing the teacher's voice only as white noise coming from somewhere beyond the boundaries of my attention, while I thought about the beating I'd had the night before, or the one I was probably going to get during the night to come.

Having been the focus of apparently loving attention at the children's home since the day I'd arrived there as a baby, I'd started to develop into an outgoing child and had always loved the company of both other children and the adults who looked after me. But by the time I started school, I'd become withdrawn and nervous, retreating increasingly into my own little world because the real world had changed so dramatically that it only bemused and distressed me. So, inevitably, as I stopped being able to concentrate on what I was supposed to be doing in the classroom, my teachers became impatient with me and with what appeared to be my wilful lack of interest and involvement in what they were trying to teach me.

The headmistress of St Patrick's was a small, grey-haired woman who used to bring her nasty, yapping, ankle-biting little dog into school every day. She didn't seem to be very fond of any of the children from Nazareth House, and the child she was least fond of was me. I suppose her dislike of me wasn't really surprising, considering how disruptive and rebellious I was becoming, but I do think she might have spared the time to wonder why I behaved the way I did. I expect she'd had a report about me from the nuns before I even started at the school, so that my unruly behaviour simply confirmed what she'd already been told.

One day, when I'd done something wrong at school – I don't remember now what it was – I was sent to the headmistress's office, where she hit me several times on the bottom with a brown leather strap. She must have reported whatever it was I'd done to the nuns, and that night I was hit again, this time on the palms of my hands with the large stainless-steel spoon that was the fear and scourge of all the children at Nazareth House, who talked about it in hushed, anxious tones and called it 'the iron spoon'.

We had just filed into the dining room for supper when I was pulled out of the line by a nun, who struck me a few times with the spoon and then told me to stand in a corner of the room.

'Face the wall and put your hands on your head,' she instructed me. 'And don't you dare move.' She waved the iron spoon in my face to emphasise her unspoken threat, and I tried very hard to look as though I didn't care.

From the corner of the room where I was standing, I could hear the clatter of cutlery and the low murmur of voices behind me. The noise was like a wave that rose slowly to a crescendo before it was quelled by the clapping of hands and by stern words from one or other of the nuns who glided between the long rows of tables and wooden benches. And then I heard the clear, high-pitched voice of my sister Teresa saying, 'Please, Sister Peter, is our Jerry going to have his dinner?'

'And what would make you think that that might be any concern of yours, Teresa Coyne?' It was clear that Sister Peter did not expect an answer to her question. But Teresa was always ready and willing to stand up for anyone she thought was being unfairly treated.

'Well, Sister Peter,' she said, in a tone that implied she considered it to be a perfectly reasonable question. 'I'm his sister, so I suppose *that* would make it my concern. And it seems to me that as he's already been punished at school for what he did, it would be a bit unfair not to let him eat his dinner.'

She was given six lashes with the spoon across the palm of her hand and then her own, half-eaten dinner was taken away. And although I couldn't see what was happening, I knew she'd be trying not to cry.

After dinner, when the children filed out of the dining room again and ran off to play, I turned around, expecting to be told that I could follow them. But it was Sister Mary who slapped the side of my head this time and told me angrily, 'Turn and face the wall, Devil's child.' Then the lights in the dining room were turned off and I was left alone in the dark.

At intervals throughout the evening, the door burst open suddenly and a beam of light fell on me where I stood in the corner of the room, my arms aching and my hands on my head. Then the door would close again, muffling once more the sound of laughter and the voices of the children playing in the playroom.

We were allowed to watch television on some evenings, although, because there were few programmes the nuns considered to be suitable for Catholic children, our viewing was always carefully monitored and controlled. Before we went to bed, we were given hot chocolate and biscuits. It was a ritual I always looked forward to – not least because I knew it was the last good thing that was going to happen to me each night. But on that particular night, there was no television, no hot chocolate and no biscuits for me.

I was so tired and my arms ached so intensely that I'd long ago begun to lower them from my head between visits from the nuns, although I hadn't yet given in to the very strong temptation to sit on the floor. Eventually though, when the door hadn't opened for what seemed like hours and there was no longer any light at all coming in through the windows above me, I must have fallen asleep where I stood, because my head suddenly jerked forward on to my chest, cricking my neck painfully and bringing me back to my senses. And, at that moment, the door burst open again and Sister Dominic came bustling into the room like an irritable penguin.

'I'd quite forgotten about you, Jerry Coyne,' she told me. 'It's way past your bedtime. Well, come along, boy. Don't dawdle.' And as she bustled out again, I ran along behind her, shaking my arms in an attempt to bring blood and life back into them.

Everyone else in the bedroom was asleep when Sister Dominic opened the door and told me to get undressed and put on my pyjamas.

'Cross your right arm over the left one and lay them on your chest,' she said. 'Then lie on your stomach.'

'B . . . b . . . but I don't want to,' I told her. 'I c . . . c . . . can't breathe with my face in the pillow.'

'But you must,' she hissed at me, leaning down so that her face was just an inch or two away from mine and I could see clearly the dark hairs on her chin. 'Because the Devil will be coming for you tonight and it's the only way you might be able to prevent him from getting inside you. And you'd better pray as hard as you can, too.'

She laughed as she walked out of the room, closing the door behind her and leaving me in the darkness.

I lay for what seemed like hours on my stomach, my arms crossed and my fists clenched as I prayed, over and over again, 'Please, Dear Lord, don't let the Devil get inside me. I'll be a good boy. I promise I will be. I don't mean to be bad. Please, Baby Jesus, don't let the Devil make me his child.'

Every sound I heard made me whimper with terror. I desperately wanted to turn over so that when the Devil came for me, I would see him as he approached my bed. But I knew that if I didn't lie on my stomach, he'd get me for sure. So I lay there, with my back exposed to the horrors of the night, just waiting and praying.

I'd needed to go the bathroom before I'd got into bed, but I'd known that asking to do so would only have made Sister Dominic even angrier than she already was. And, of course, after she left the room, there was absolutely no chance I was going to get out of bed again – and risk meeting the Devil in the toilet. So, eventually, as the minutes and then the hours ticked slowly by, I wet the bed.

In the morning, I thought I'd been awake all night, although I suppose I must have fallen asleep at some point. But although I was tired and my eyes were red and sore, I was filled with relief and almost a sense of pride. I could hardly believe I was safe and that I'd made it through the night and kept the Devil away with my prayers. Maybe God could hear me after all, and He hadn't abandoned me because of my terrible, wicked sins.

I should have known, though, that being saved from one nightmare meant only that I'd increased my chances of falling victim to the next, and while I was standing beside my bed wondering what to do with the wet pyjamas I'd just taken off, Sister Dominic came into the room. She was followed by two other nuns and she looked even angrier than she usually did. Without saying a word, she strode across the room towards me, reached out her stubby-fingered hand and grabbed hold of my penis.

'Devil's child! Devil's child!' she shouted at me, pulling me down on to the floor so that I cried out in pain. 'I will beat the Devil out of you if it's the last thing I do, you evil, evil boy.'

'But I kept my arms crossed all night,' I whispered between my sobs. 'I did exactly what you told me to do.

I lay on my stomach and I prayed as hard as I could. I'm sure I only fell asleep for a minute. The Devil couldn't have got inside me. Please, Sister Dominic. I'm telling you the truth. I promise.'

'Go to the bathroom and get washed,' she snapped, bending down to punch me in the groin as I lay whimpering on the floor beside my bed. 'And don't look in the mirror, ugly boy.'

A few days later, I punched a boy at school when he called me a bastard and taunted me for having no parents. We were in the playground and the deputy head saw what happened and dragged me by my ear to the headmistress's office, where I was told to lie across her desk and was beaten with a leather strap. Afterwards, when the skin on my bottom was so raw and painful I could hardly walk, I was made to stand in a corner of the dining room while the other children ate their lunch.

That afternoon, I sat silently on the bus, wishing and praying that something – anything – would happen to prevent it arriving at Nazareth House. Once again though, God didn't hear me, and I slunk through the front door behind the other children with my head down, like a miserable, submissive dog that knows it's in for a kicking.

To my amazement, however, nothing was said to me by any of the nuns, and as I ate my supper, went out to play, had my bath, said my prayers and went to bed, my sense of relief continued to grow. The headmistress must have decided that the beating she gave me was punishment enough for what I'd done and so she hadn't told Mother Superior about it. I couldn't believe my luck, and that night I added another, private prayer to the ones we'd learned to say, thanking God for his mercy and telling him I hadn't meant to be bad, but that I hated it when the other children teased and bullied me because I didn't have parents who loved me and a nice home, like they did.

I don't know what time it was when I woke up to find two nuns standing beside my bed.

'Get up and go to the toilet,' one of them whispered to me. 'We don't want you wetting your bed again, do we?'

Still dazed by sleep, I slid my legs over the side of the bed and touched the cold floor with my bare feet. The nuns followed me as I padded out of the room and along the corridor towards the toilets. But as I lifted my arm to turn the handle and go in, one of them said, in a low, quiet voice, 'No, not in there. Those toilets are broken. You'll have to use some other ones. Follow me.'

I stumbled sleepily along behind the nuns until we reached the part of the building where the old people lived, where we stopped by the door of a room I hadn't ever been into before.

I was inside it and the door had been closed behind me by the time I realised it wasn't a toilet. On the wall opposite me was a large crucifix, and underneath it were three or four nuns, just standing there looking at me. I tried to make a run for it, swinging round and grabbing for the door handle, but a strong hand closed around my arm and then other hands began to pull at me and lift me off the ground.

I fought back, kicking out wildly and making contact with the body of at least one of my assailants. But I was just a child – a particularly scrawny one, even for my young age – and I didn't stand a chance.

Suddenly, the nuns let go of me and my body dropped like a stone to the floor.

'It seems you need to be taught a lesson,' one of them said, leaning down towards me so that I could feel her spit on my face. 'How dare you bring disgrace on us by fighting at school?' She kicked me as she said the last word and, as though her action was the signal the other nuns had been waiting for, they all began to slap me and kick me too.

As I lay on the rough, cold flagstones at their feet, someone stamped on my leg and I cried out and tried to curl my body into a ball, clasping my hands behind my head and pressing my elbows together in front of my face in an attempt to protect it from their assault.

'Devil's child,' the nuns chanted as they hit me. And I knew they must be right.

Then, as abruptly as it had begun, their attack stopped and for a moment the room was silent, except for the rasping sound made by the nuns as they tried to catch their breath after their exertions. I was still curled up and my whole body was shaking when I was lifted off the floor and thrown on to a bed in the centre of the room. And as I lay there on my back, pinned to the mattress by two nuns who were holding my arms and legs, the others continued to slap and punch me.

'It doesn't hurt,' I yelled at them through my tears. 'You're all fucking evil bastards. *You're* the Devil's children. I hate you.' It was as though I'd reached some sort of breaking point, and although it *did* hurt, more than anything had ever hurt me before, in that moment my hatred of the nuns was even stronger than the pain.

I felt something around my neck and I began to struggle, fighting for breath, but only succeeding in tightening whatever it was that was choking me, until it seemed as though all the energy was flowing out of my body and my life was slipping away.

Half conscious and no longer trying to resist what was being done to me, I heard someone say, 'Stop! That's enough. You'll kill him. This is madness. He's only a child.' And the next thing I knew, I was lying on a bed, cradled in the arms of a nun I'd never seen before, in an otherwise empty room.

'I'm sorry, child. I'm so sorry,' she kept saying, and as she rocked me backwards and forwards like a baby, tears filled her pale-blue eyes and spilled out on to her cheeks. Then she carried me back along the corridor to my room, where she lay me down gently on my bed, covered me with blankets and sat beside me, her rosary beads clasped tightly in her hands, until I fell asleep.

That night I had some of the most horrible, terrifying nightmares I'd ever had, and when I woke up in the morning, the nun had gone and I never saw her again.

# Chapter Three

I had no memory of my mother, and I rarely thought about her, except when she sent me a birthday card, which she did every year. I was given the envelope after school and a nun would stand beside me while I opened it, holding out her hand for the £5 note which was always tucked inside the card and which she'd take – 'for safe keeping'. I never saw any of those £5 notes again, but it didn't really matter, because what was really important to me was the card itself, or, more specifically, the words that were written inside it:

To my darling son Jerry
Happy birthday
From your loving Mammy
xxxxxx

They were the same words every year, and every year I'd read them over and over again before counting the kisses and trying to remember how many there'd been on my last card.

I didn't even know what my mother looked like, and I did sometimes wonder why, if I had a mother who loved me – as she said she did in her cards – I was living in a home with orphans and children who'd been abandoned by their presumably unloving parents.

When you're a child in a children's home and your life is intensely miserable and confusing, every scrap of love, however vague and unsubstantiated, is important to you. So I didn't like to think too much about the apparent contradiction between what my mother wrote and what she did, in case I came to a conclusion I'd rather not have to face. Instead, I just accepted her written words of love, as I'd gladly have accepted the lick of a dog on my face, as a sign of the affection I craved.

Eventually, my mother made contact with the Catholic Children's Society – the charity responsible for the care of five of her six children – and came to visit us. She only came a handful of times during my entire childhood, and she never stayed long. She didn't seem to want to know about our lives; instead, she talked about her own, about how hard she worked, how expensive it was to live in London, and how the two-hour train journey to Nottingham had tired her out.

At the time, we were too young and too grateful for

the fact that she'd come at all to feel anything but adoration for her as she sat there in her expensive-looking clothes, blowing the smoke from her cigarette over the tops of our heads. We felt sorry for her, too, when she sighed and told us how she longed to be able to move back to Nottingham so that she could be with us again.

After one of her visits, when we'd walked with her to the railway station and were sitting on the platform, waiting with her for her train, she said she hated London and the horrible, cold house she lived in, and that she had no friends and never went out anywhere except to work. We cried as we listened to her, and again as we waved her off on the train. But, in fact, my tears weren't really for my mother; they were for Geraldine, because *she* was sobbing and I hated to see her upset. In my eyes, Geraldine was my *real* mother – the person who was always there for me, who wiped away my tears when I cried and who kissed and cuddled me and made me feel better when I hurt myself or when I was sad and couldn't tell her why.

And I'm glad now that I didn't waste much sympathy on my mother, because her life turned out to be very different from the lonely, miserable one she described to us during the brief afternoon visits she made every couple of years to Nazareth House.

One day, when I was six years old, my mother came to see us and told us that as soon as she'd settled into a new house in the area of London she'd moved to, she was going to come back to Nottingham to get us. I was almost ecstatic with excitement. It seemed that all my prayers were going to be answered, because although I didn't have much true feeling for my mother, the one thing above all else that I longed to do was get away from Nazareth House. I'd realised by that time that not all children lived in children's homes with nuns who were always angry with them and who woke them up in the middle of the night to beat them. And now I was going to be one of the lucky ones, with a proper house, a mother and a real family.

'It'll be any day now,' I kept telling myself after my mother had left again on the train. 'Mum will come for us and we'll all go with her to London and be together. I don't suppose there'll be enough rooms for us to have one each, so I'll probably have to share a bedroom with John.' The thought of it sent me jigging around the room in a dance of uncontainable joy.

When the nuns realised how excited I was, they took great pleasure in telling me, 'Your mother's never going to come for you. It's never going to happen. Nobody wants you. Why would anyone want the Devil's child?' Then they laughed in a spiteful, sneering way that made me want to pick something up and hurl it across the room or smash my fists into the wall.

But they were right, of course. Although she repeated

her promise several times over the next few years, our mother never did come for us, and I don't think she ever had any intention of doing so. So I tried to comfort myself with the thought that, although I might not see them very often, at least my brother and sisters were living in the children's home with me, and that was almost like having a proper family.

My oldest sister, Geraldine, had become our surrogate mother when she was just seven, which meant she always had to be old beyond her years and never had a real childhood at all. She was the spokesperson for all of us, and she watched out for us, although she didn't ever need to worry about John.

John was the nuns' favourite and he had very little contact with the rest of us. In fact, I don't remember him ever playing with me like my sisters did, and I sometimes forgot he was my brother, although I always looked up to him and admired him and wished I could do something to make him notice me and be proud of me. Sadly, though, as I became more disturbed and my behaviour deteriorated, the only attention I attracted from anyone was negative, and I could understand why John seemed to want to pretend he had no connection with me.

My sister Carmella had been three when our mother left and we were taken into care, and the nuns seemed to hate her almost as much as they hated me. There wasn't a great deal that Geraldine could do to protect me; she had her hands full trying to keep Carmella out of trouble and out of the way of the nuns.

And then there was my sister Teresa, who was just two when I was born and who I think must have been put into another group of children at Nazareth House, because I rarely saw her and I can't remember ever spending much time with her. In fact, I didn't really spend much time with any of my siblings, which – in view of the trouble that followed me wherever I went – must have seemed to them like a blessing.

John was always busy doing something, and the nuns gave him a patch of ground at the side of the laundry, which he made into a little garden. He would dig, plant and water for hours on end, and I'd often stand at a window watching him, feeling proud to have a brother everyone loved, who could make things grow and had responsibilities like a man. Sometimes I'd bang on the window and John would look up and wave, and then I'd literally jump up and down with happiness. And sometimes I'd point him out to other people, tapping on the window with my fingers as I told them, 'That's my brother, John. He made that garden, and I'm going to make one too, when I'm older.' I longed to go outside and help him, or just stand beside him and bask in the glory of being related to such a wonderful person. But I wasn't allowed to: John was good and I was bad, and the nuns did not want to encourage the link between us.

It was true that I did seem increasingly to do things that caused trouble, and I could sense John's lack of eagerness to be associated with me. For example, there was one day when I got into a fight with another boy at Nazareth House. To begin with, the other boy was winning and was on top of me, both fists flailing as he punched me repeatedly, raining blows down on my head until I felt dizzy. But then, somehow, I managed to get the upper hand, and just as I'd hit him squarely on the jaw, John walked up to me and punched me on the side of the face with such force that I was sent flying through the air.

For a moment, I just sat there on the ground, touching my face and looking up at John in disbelief. He was my brother. He should have protected me, not taken someone else's side against me. And then two nuns and a member of the lay staff came running out to see what was happening, and John told them he'd hit me because I'd attacked the other boy.

A small crowd of onlookers had gathered around us, but I could see only John. With my eyes filled with tears of shocked hurt, I told him, 'But he punched me first. I didn't hit him till he'd hit me lots of times.'

Of course, no one believed me. John had accused me,

and I knew there was no way in the world anyone was going to take my word against his.

It was only the middle of the afternoon, but I was sent to my bedroom, where I sat on my bed, wiping away the blood that was still dripping from my nose and occasionally touching the site of the fierce, throbbing pain in the side of my head.

I'd probably been sitting there for about an hour when the door opened and three nuns came into the room. One of them was holding a slipper and another had a brown leather sandal in her outstretched hand. I stifled a sob at the thought of what was about to happen, and then suddenly I felt weary, because I was helpless and because I didn't have anyone who would stand up for me and take my side against the world.

Two of the nuns grabbed me and threw me, face down, on to the bed. I reached out to lock my fingers around the metal rails of the bed-head and, this time, I didn't even struggle as my shorts and pants were pulled down, although I did shout out when I felt the first stinging blow across the tender skin of my bottom. Immediately, one of the nuns pushed my face down into the pillow to muffle my screams and another sat on my legs to stop me kicking out again as one vicious blow followed another.

My whole body was shuddering. I couldn't breathe and I began to panic. I gagged and almost vomited as the coarse white material of the pillowcase filled my mouth. Then, just as I thought I was going to choke and die, I was released. I lifted my head from the pillow and took a huge gulp of air, like a diver raising himself out of the water, and the nun holding the leather sandal waved it in my face and said, 'I *will* beat the Devil out of you, as God is my witness.' Her own face was bright red – as mine must have been too – and she was panting. But she still had enough energy to hit me across the side of the head with the sandal, so hard that I was knocked off the bed and fell on the floor, clutching my hand to the red-hot-poker pain in my ear.

I crawled towards the corner of the room and tried to curl myself into a ball. But the nuns had already encircled me and they began to lash out at me, kicking me as I attempted to struggle to my feet in the hope of making a dash for the door. I'd forgotten that my shorts and pants were still around my ankles, and as I tripped and fell headlong, I banged my head against the side of the bed, almost knocking myself out.

There was a pulsating pain in my ear and a sick dizziness threatened to overwhelm me as I got to my feet again, pulled up my shorts and pants and ran out of the bedroom, down the stairs and through the open front door.

John was still playing with the other children in the yard outside, and I stood watching him for a moment.

Although he had his back to me, I could have called out his name and asked him to help me. But I knew there was no point: *he* was the one who'd got me into trouble in the first place – whether deliberately or not, I didn't know. I needed to find my sister Geraldine. She'd protect me, whatever she thought I'd done.

I quickly scanned the yard, but I couldn't see her, and I knew the nuns would be close behind me. So I ran to the small, flat-roofed building that housed the laundry and hid there until one of the workers eventually came in and sent me to join the other children for tea in the dining room, where, to my surprise and relief, nothing more was said about what had happened.

As a result of those incidents – and others – I realised that John didn't have any real love or brotherly feelings for me. I still admired him though, and sometimes, when I was daydreaming, I imagined him putting his arm around my shoulders and saying proudly to people, 'This is my kid brother, Jerry.'

Occasionally, Dad visited us at Nazareth House. I don't think he really wanted to come, but I suppose he had to pretend from time to time to be interested in us and in what happened to us. After all, he was getting a good deal: one of his sons was in an institution, with the cost of his care being met by the state, and his other five children were being looked after by the Catholic Children's Society, leaving him free to indulge his love of booze, birds and blarney, or whatever else occupied his time. I never felt comfortable with my father though – I don't think any of his children did – and I always stayed close to Geraldine when he was around.

I remember one day when he came to visit us while we were playing in University Park, where the nuns sometimes took the children during the summer holidays. It was a beautiful park, with grass that was greener than any I'd ever seen before, a boating lake, a paddling pool and a stream you could wade into in your bare feet and where you could catch little fish in a net. The nuns would take sandwiches and oranges as lunch for all the children and we'd stay at the park for what seemed like hours, roaming around and doing whatever we wanted to do. I loved those days, not least because of the taste of freedom and normality they gave me.

At first, I didn't recognise my own father when I saw him walking across the grass towards us, which I suppose was partly because his presence there was so unexpected. On the rare occasions when he could spare a few minutes to spend with us, he was always determined to show the nuns that he was a man who cared about his children and was nice to them when he *did* see them. But he seemed awkward and ill at ease as he strode up to us that day and asked, 'Now, who would like to be treated to an ice cream?'

His voice was jovial, although his smile seemed forced, but I'd already decided I didn't really like or trust him and I shook my head. I was scared of him too, although I didn't understand why at the time. And I resented the fact that I was living in a children's home, being regularly beaten and abused by the nuns, while he seemed to think that all he had to do to absolve himself from any real responsibility towards us and show he was 'good father' was drop in a couple of times a year and buy us an ice cream.

I shook my head again, silently, and he glanced quickly towards where the nuns were sitting on benches beside the duck pond before reaching out his hand to pinch my cheek and roar in bluff amazement, 'No ice cream?' But although his smile was broad, the expression in his eyes was cold. 'Did you ever hear of a child who turned down the offer of an ice cream?' He raised his eyebrows and looked at Geraldine, who laughed nervously. Then he grabbed me, pulling me down on to the grass and tickling me as he roared again, 'No ice cream, is it? Whoever heard of such a thing?'

But although John, Geraldine, Carmella and Teresa all accepted his offer and thanked him politely, I was determined not to be cajoled and humoured into taking anything from him that might make him think I'd forgiven him – or would ever forgive him – for abandoning us the way he had. However much I might have wanted to have a father who played with me in the park and bought me treats – and I *did* want those things, more than anything I'd ever wanted in my life – the reality was that I was living in a home for orphans, waifs and strays, where I was unhappy and badly treated. So whatever he offered me, I wasn't going to play along with him and make him feel better about having abandoned me. I *wanted* him to feel bad and to be sorry, because however bad he felt, I knew he'd never, ever come anywhere close to knowing what it felt like to be me.

He'd only been with us in the park for maybe twenty minutes when suddenly, without any word of explanation, he jumped to his feet and began to run across the grass towards the gates. John, Geraldine, Carmella, Teresa and I watched in open-mouthed astonishment as he darted out on to the pavement and leapt on to a bus – presumably because he'd just realised what time it was and that the pubs would soon be opening. He didn't say goodbye to us or even look in our direction as the bus drove away down the road, and it felt like a hollow victory to know I'd been right not to trust him or to believe he really cared about anyone but himself.

Then, one day, I walked down the stairs at Nazareth House and found my father standing in the hallway with John, Geraldine and Carmella. Carmella was stamping her foot, waving her arms in the air and shouting, and although I couldn't make out what she was saying, her anger seemed to be directed towards two nuns, who were watching her impassively.

I'd stopped a few stairs from the bottom, and as one of the nuns turned to John, I heard her say quietly, 'But surely *you* don't want to leave with your sisters?' She smiled at him as she spoke, holding out her hands towards him in a beseeching gesture, and John answered solemnly, 'I think it's my duty.'

I jumped down the last few stairs and ran towards them, asking excitedly, 'Leaving? Who's leaving? What's happening?'

'Your father has come to take his children to live with him at home,' one of the nuns answered coldly. She snatched at my shoulder, but I twisted away from her, avoiding her grasp, and asked again, 'But who's leaving?'

Without answering, or even looking in my direction, John thanked the nuns for everything they'd done for him and told them, 'I'll miss everyone here and I'm very grateful to all of you.' And although he was just twelve years old, he sounded like a man. Then he picked up a suitcase from the floor beside him and walked towards the front door, followed, without a backward glance, by Geraldine, Carmella and my father.

'Wait!' I shouted. But none of them gave any sign of even being aware that I was there.

My heart was racing and I had the same horrible, full-up feeling I often had when something bad was about to happen. I looked from one nun to the other as I asked, 'Aren't I going with them?' And, finally, they seemed to notice me.

The nun nearest to me grabbed me by the hair, dragging me away from the door, and said, 'And why would they want someone like you? No one wants *you*.' Then she slapped the back of my head and I had one last glimpse of my family as they walked away from me, before the front door was closed behind them.

Teresa had been left behind too, for reasons I never found out. But as she was in a different group from the one I was in and I rarely saw her anyway, it was a fact that gave me little comfort. I was seven years old, frightened, unloved and, it seemed, unlovable; so perhaps it wasn't surprising that I was developing an apparently tough protective shell in an unconscious attempt to cut myself off emotionally from the many things that bemused and hurt me. Often though, not even that was enough to contain the anger that sometimes burst out of me at the slightest provocation.

As the days passed, I missed my brother and sisters more and more. Geraldine had always watched over me, even if only from a distance, and Carmella had been loud in her support of me. And now I was on my own, separated from anyone who might really care about me, and I was lonely. I wondered if I'd ever see my siblings again, and then I began to wonder if they even *wanted* to see *me*.

I'd lie in bed at night thinking about them while I waited for the nuns to come and drag me to the 'beating room', where I was still regularly punished for being – unwittingly and unwillingly – the Devil's child, and where Jesus looked down impassively from the crucifix on the wall. I often imagined my brother and sisters sitting around a table in a brightly lit room, talking and laughing as they ate their dinner with our dad. In the picture I could see in my mind, they had a dog – I'd always longed to have a dog – and Carmella sneaked food to him under the table when no one was looking.

*It must be grand*, I thought, *to be a proper family. They must be having a great time.*

One day, I asked a nun who was usually less unkind to me than most of the others when I would be able to see my brother and sisters again. But she just smacked the back of my head and told me to go away and not be silly, which didn't seem to be any sort of answer at all.

Inevitably, I suppose, the bonds between me and my siblings began to weaken and the void that was left in my heart slowly filled with resentment. It was clear to me that, just like my father and my mother, they had abandoned me because they didn't want me and because they had never really cared about me. It was an incredibly painful realisation, and what hurt most of all was that not even Geraldine wanted to see me.

Geraldine had been the only 'mother' I'd ever known and, until the day she left with my father, I'd accepted without question the fact that she loved me. But it seemed I'd been wrong, because as soon as she'd had the chance to escape, she'd taken it and gone without me. It felt as though a door had slammed shut, cutting me off from the one small zone of safety that had always existed in my life.

John came back to Nazareth House on many occasions after he'd left, although the purpose of his visits was never to see me, and sometimes I didn't even know he'd been there until someone told me after he'd gone. John had always been good with his hands. When he'd lived in the children's home, he'd made go-karts and fixed up bikes for several boys, repairing them with bits from other old bikes he'd dismantled and then re-spraying their frames so they looked like new. And that's what he continued to do on the days when he came back.

And then, one day, while he was there on a visit and I was standing in the bike shed watching him working, he suddenly asked me, 'Have you got a bike, Jerry?' I held my breath as I answered 'no', and he looked at me for a moment before bending down and pulling out an old bike frame from a stack that was leaning against the wall of the shed. Then he took a couple of bits of what looked like rusty metal off a shelf and held them up to the light to examine them.

'Well, there seems to be plenty of stuff here,' he said, and when he glanced at me this time, he almost smiled. 'I'll start on it next week.'

I thought I was going to faint with excitement. What colour would he spray it? And, even more importantly, how was I going to make sure everyone knew that my bike had been made for me by my very own brother, who was cleverer than any other brother in the whole world?

Every time John visited Nazareth House over the next few weeks, I stood in the bike shed watching him as he cleaned and sanded bits from broken, battered bikes, screwed them on to the frame he'd selected and then sprayed my bike bright red. I hadn't dared to ask him what colour it was going to be, in case I annoyed him, but it seemed that God had actually been listening when I'd offered up that particular prayer.

After John had fixed some wheels to the frame, pumped up the tyres and adjusted the brakes, my bicycle was almost ready to go. At last, I was going to be able to ride around with all the other kids with bikes, which meant I'd be the one thing I'd always longed to be: part of a group.

I knew the other children were getting sick of my bragging about how my brother was making me a bike and that it was probably the best bike anyone had ever seen, or was ever likely to see. But the happiness I felt was unlike any feeling I'd ever had before, and I couldn't stop myself. On one occasion, when I'd been shouting my mouth off yet again, another boy claimed John was actually making the bike for him. But instead of flying into a rage, as I might have done previously, I just laughed in his face and told him he was jealous.

And then, one Saturday morning, I looked out of the window of the dining room after breakfast and saw the other boy riding my beautiful red bicycle around the yard.

As I ran out of the front door, I could hear his whoops of delight and I could see my brother John standing at the edge of the yard, watching him and smiling. It felt as though someone had punched me in the stomach. But I knew I mustn't cry and let everyone see that I was upset, so I stood there silently as the boy jumped off the bike, thumped John on the arm and shouted excitedly, 'Thanks, John. It's really great.'

I felt completely numb. Despite my best efforts to hold them back, the tears began to pour down my cheeks, and that's when one of the other children noticed me standing there. Pointing at me, he laughed and began to taunt me, saying, in a cruel, exaggerated impersonation of my voice, 'Oh, my brother John is making a new bike specially for me. Did I tell you that John is my brother? It's a red bike, you know, and it's just for me, made for me by my brother John.'

I looked at John, but he didn't turn his head to look at me, and in that moment I hated him. I ran back into the house and up the stairs to my bedroom, where I crawled under my bed and sobbed until there were no tears left in my body.

I did ask John about that incident a few years later, and about why he'd promised to make me a bicycle and had then given it to someone else. But he said he couldn't remember it, and that I must have made a mistake when I thought the bike was for me. Maybe I *did* make a mistake. It doesn't matter now, although the sense of betrayal and soul-destroying disappointment I felt that day has stayed with me ever since. I was seven years old and very unhappy, and my perception of what had happened was just another indication of the fact that there was something wrong with me, something that made God ignore my prayers and punish me because I was undeserving of anything good in life, including, most importantly of all, the right to be loved.

# Chapter Four

My eyes flicked open. I didn't know if I'd actually been asleep, but I was sure I'd heard a noise. I lay completely still – on my back with my arms crossed over my chest, as the nuns always insisted we should lie – and I listened.

It was too dark to see anything other than the vague outlines of the other beds and the few bits of utilitarian furniture in the bedroom, but I could definitely hear the hushed whispering of at least two voices. It seemed to be coming from directly outside the bedroom door. I thought I heard someone say my name and then everything went quiet.

My heart was thumping and my fists were clenched so tightly my fingernails were digging painfully into the palms of my hands, because I knew that even if they'd gone, they'd be back for me. Although the trauma of night-time beatings hadn't diminished in any way, I'd almost learned to accept them as part of my life and even to close my mind to them while they were actually happening, so that I could try to imagine I was somewhere else. For some reason though, I had a very bad feeling about what was going to happen that night, and I was frightened.

My brain was telling me to hide or run away. But there was no point doing anything except wait, because there was nowhere to hide and nowhere to run to. So I just lay on my back in my bed, with my head raised slightly off the pillow as I strained to listen, and waited. My stomach was churning and the slightest noise – one of the other children moaning in their sleep or turning over in bed – made the saliva rush into my mouth so that I thought I was going to vomit.

I was so tense with fear that it was almost a relief when the bedroom door slowly opened and two nuns seemed to glide into the room. I shut my eyes quickly and made a small, unconvincing snoring noise each time I breathed in. One of the nuns leaned over me, and as I felt her breath on my face, I had to force myself to keep my eyes closed. Then a strong, stubby finger poked me in the chest and she whispered, 'Get up. Get up, Jerry, and put on your dressing gown. You're going to serve on the altar. Hurry now.'

The nuns waited while I got out of bed and struggled into my dressing gown, and then they ushered me silently out of the room into the corridor, where one of them grasped my elbow and asked me, 'Are you ready?'

'Yes,' I told her, but before I had a chance to voice the question that was in my head, she held a finger to her lips and began to push me along the corridor in front of her.

Although I'd served on the altar in the chapel in the grounds of Nazareth House many times, I'd never before had to do it in my nightclothes in the middle of the night. So I knew something else was about to happen, and as I scurried down the corridor ahead of the nuns, my fear seemed to form a solid lump in my stomach.

I didn't have any idea what time it was until we passed a clock on the wall in one of the silent, dimly lit hallways on the way to the chapel and I realised it was 2 o'clock in the morning. I stopped walking and turned to look at the nuns, and as one of them reached out her hand to grip my arm, I said, 'But it's too early for chapel. I don't understand. Why would . . .?'

'Just do as you're told,' she hissed at me, squeezing my elbow with her bony fingers and pushing me on down the corridor.

As we walked through the part of the building where the old people lived, I could hear the rumble of snores and the occasional creak of a bedspring, and for a moment I considered shouting out in the hope of waking someone up. I liked some of the old people, and I'd sometimes sit on a stool beside the chair of one old lady listening, entranced, to the stories she told about what the world had been like when she was young. But I'd rarely seen any of them take more than a few uncertain steps unsupported, so they were hardly going to come rushing out of their bedrooms to save me, and as soon as the thought entered my head, I realised it was a stupid idea.

Eventually, we stopped outside the door of a room I'd been taken to for a beating once before, although this time when I stepped inside and the door closed behind me, I was alone. It wasn't long, though, before five or six nuns filed into the room in silence and stood in a circle around me. I didn't look at their faces, because my eyes were fixed on the sticks, slippers and large metal spoons they were holding in their hands. When I'd entered the room, the bed had been pushed up against a wall, but now two of the nuns lifted it into the centre of the room and I was told to lie down on it.

It didn't even cross my mind to argue or protest, because I knew I was completely powerless – a terrified little boy against half a dozen determinedly cruel, self-righteous adults who were given added strength by the conviction that they were doing God's work. There was nothing I could do to change the course of the events that were about to take place, so the sooner the beating was over, the sooner I could return to my bed and be left to sleep undisturbed – for the rest of that night, at least.

As I lay on the bed, the door opened again and more

nuns came into the room. My hands were tied to the metal bed-head, a piece of material was forced into my mouth and the nuns began to pray for my soul. I couldn't control the shivering of my body, but I was determined not to show my fear in any other way. Perhaps the nuns were right and what they were about to do to me *was* God's will. What did I know compared to them? But there was one thing I did know by that time, which was that, although I still believed in God and the Devil, there wasn't much to choose between them.

The nuns seemed to have been praying for hours by the time they finally stopped, although in reality it was probably just a few minutes. Someone had brought a tray of plastic jugs into the room and I watched warily as they passed them to each other, wondering what they were going to do. Then, suddenly, they started to pour water over my face. Because of the gag in my mouth, I had to breathe through my nose, and even that became almost impossible when I panicked.

I began to shake my head wildly from side to side, and by the time the jugs were empty and the nuns had stopped pouring water over me, I felt as though my lungs were about to burst. I was still gasping for breath when one of the nuns bent down and pulled my shoulders off the bed, while another slipped a pillowcase over my head. Instantly, my fear turned to terror. I began to struggle and as I lashed out with my feet, I felt a weight on my legs as one of the nuns pinned them to the bed.

As blows rained down on every part of my body, the pain was far worse than any I'd ever felt before. I tried to draw air into my lungs so that I could scream, but as I did so, the gag moved further into my mouth, making me choke and forcing the scream back inside me – where I sometimes think it still is today, reverberating and echoing endlessly, unheard by anyone except me. Then, suddenly, it felt as though the fear was draining out of me. I stopped struggling and just lay there, still and silent, with my mind completely empty.

Gradually, the room became quiet too, until the only sound I could hear was the deep, rapid breathing of the nuns. When someone lifted the pillowcase off my head, one of the nuns bent down and slapped my face. I blinked and as I looked up at her, I could see in her eyes an expression of almost frenzied hatred.

'You are the Devil's child,' she hissed at me, pulling the material roughly from my mouth. 'Go on, say it. Say "I am the Devil's child".'

'I am the Devil's child,' I told her, and as I said the words I knew they must be true, because I could think of no other explanation as to why God would let the nuns hurt me the way they did.

The nun was still looking down at me with disgust

when I felt a sudden rush of anger, like a hot liquid flooding through every part of my body, and I shouted into her face, 'And you are the Devil's fucking mother.'

I don't know where the words came from. I regretted them as soon as I'd said them, and I was right to be afraid. The nun's eyes seemed to bulge and her face turned from red to purple as she slapped me again and said, in a low, coldly menacing voice, 'All right then. We'll do this the hard way, if that's what you want.'

The pillowcase was put back over my head, my hands were untied from the bed-head and I was lifted off the bed on to my feet. My one foolish moment of bravado had passed as quickly as it had come, and I was close to panic as I asked, 'Where are we going?'

'Well, *you* are going to hell,' a voice answered. 'I don't think there's any question about that.'

With my arms held by one of the nuns, I was pushed out of the room and pulled along corridors, down stairs and through the front door of the building into the cool night air. I'd been at Nazareth House since I was three months old and I knew the buildings and the grounds pretty well, so I could tell where we were as we walked through the rose garden, past the workmen's shed and into the nuns' graveyard with its neat rows of graves under the trees.

I started struggling and kicking out with my feet, which

only resulted in more hands gripping my body until I was being held so tightly I could no longer move at all. Then the pillowcase was lifted off my head and I looked down into a deep, black hole in the ground. My feet were right at the edge of an open grave and as I screamed and tried to step backwards away from it, the nuns pushed me even further forward.

'Throw him in,' one of them said.

'No, please,' I whimpered, trying again to take a step away from the grave. My whole body was shaking and I could feel the trickle of liquid running down the inside of my legs. 'Please, please, don't throw me in.' I was sobbing and stuttering so badly the words were barely understandable. 'I'll try harder. I *won't* let the Devil in. I promise. Please.'

I was pushing against the nuns, but they were holding me so tightly that instead of moving away from the grave, my feet were slipping closer to it, until, for one terrifying moment, I seemed to be dangling above the open ground. I screamed again and began to shout hysterically, 'No, please. I'm sorry. I'm sorry.' And then I was falling, tumbling into the darkness, my mind completely paralysed by fear.

There was a shallow layer of water at the bottom of the grave and the muddy soil beneath it sucked at my feet when I tried to stand up. Soil was still falling on me from above too, and when I looked up, I realised that the nuns were pushing the earth down on top of me.

Moaning and sobbing pathetically, I scrabbled at the sides of the grave with my hands, trying to claw my way up it. Then I began to jump, hoping that, by some miracle, I'd be able to reach the top and grab hold of solid ground with my fingertips. But the hole was much too deep and I was being blinded by the soil that was falling into my eyes from above. So I stopped jumping, and bent over just in time before I was sick.

When I stood upright again, I took a step forward to try to steady myself, and as I did so I slipped and fell, so that the vomit stuck to the mud that was already soaking through my dressing gown and forming a cold, foul-smelling layer on my trembling body. I was more frightened than I had ever been in my life. But as the last of my energy drained out of me, the fear seemed to fade too, and I lay for a moment at the bottom of that grave, feeling as though my brain had become overloaded and my head was slowly filling with the same darkness that surrounded me.

I must have passed out, because the next thing I knew, I was being lifted to my feet and my hands were being held in place on the rungs of a ladder, which had been lowered from above. I clambered up it as quickly as I could, step by step, towards where the nuns were still

Jerry Coyne

grouped together, muttering and glaring at me, apparently without one single scrap of humanity or sympathy to share amongst them.

'It would have been better to bury him,' one of them said, looking at me with an expression of undisguised disgust. 'It would have been better for God's world to be rid of the Devil's child.'

But instead of burying me alive, they took me – still covered in mud and stinking of vomit – to the chapel, where I was told to kneel in front of the altar and pray to almighty and merciful God for his forgiveness. I can remember looking up at the crucifix on the wall above my head and thinking, *Is there really a God? If there is, why does he hate me and allow such terrible things to happen to me? And if I pray really, really hard and he* does *forgive me and make me good, will* I *ever be able to forgive the nuns?*

Although my faith in God had been severely shaken and the first seeds of doubt about His existence had been implanted in my mind, I still felt embarrassed to be kneeling in His house in such a filthy state. It seemed that the nuns shared my revulsion, because after I'd been praying for a while, one of them appeared with a bucket of water and a mop, which she pushed into my hands as she said, 'Look at the dirt you've brought into God's sacred house, filthy child. Clean it up this minute.'

Some of the nuns had gone, but a few of them waited while I mopped the chapel floor. When I'd finished, they led me to a bathroom in the old people's part of the building, where they took away my pyjamas and dressing gown and told me to get into a bath that was half full of ice-cold, yellow water. The smell of disinfectant was over-powering as I stepped into the bathtub, and I stood there with my teeth chattering until one of the nuns tugged on my arm to make me sit down and I fell, banging my head against the side.

Two of the nuns scrubbed my shaking body with nail-brushes until it felt as though every inch of my skin had been peeled off, bit by painful bit. When I whispered, 'It hurts,' one of them slapped my head and said angrily, 'Of course it hurts to have the Devil scrubbed out of you.'

Later, as I climbed into bed, a nun warned me, in a low, quiet voice, 'If you breathe a word about what happened to you tonight, you *will* be buried alive next time.' Then she left the room and, finally alone, I lay awake for what remained of the night, staring at the changing colours on the ceiling and trying to pray to God, although, for some reason, I couldn't think of any words to say to Him.

Thirty-five years later, I still have nightmares about what happened to me that night, as well as flashbacks that are so real my heart starts to thud and I feel the same fear and can smell the sour odour of wet earth, vomit and disinfectant. I know those memories will be with me for the rest of my life; there's nothing I can do about that. Something died inside me that night and although part of me wants to be able to forgive the nuns, I can't. I hate them.

I was a little boy who had been abandoned by his parents and wasn't loved by anyone. I didn't realise it at the time, but it was that sense of being unloved and unlovable that underlined my cheekiness and what the nuns considered to be my 'bad behaviour' – which was, in reality, little more than occasional outbursts of childish defiance.

But I was just a child, for God's sake – a child with two parents who didn't want him and who'd left him in a children's home, for reasons I didn't understand then and have finally had to accept I'll never really comprehend. What I do know now, though, is that the problems that caused my parents to desert me and my siblings lay within *them* and weren't my fault – and, despite the fact that the harm has already been done and it's too late to fix my damaged 'inner child', that is comforting to know.

Of course, the other kids took their cue from the nuns and simply accepted my 'bad character' as a fact – which it eventually started to become, as I struggled to express the resentment and confusion that were building up inside me. So, always one to try my best to make a virtue out of a necessity, I began to enjoy my own company. Perhaps the other children *didn't* like me, or perhaps they were just keen to earn favour with the nuns by reporting to them my slightest transgression. I don't know which explanation was true; I just soon learned to accept that it was best to avoid them.

It turned out that I wasn't the only child who was being badly treated by the nuns – which came as a huge surprise to me, because although I hated them, I'd never really considered the possibility that they were 'wrong' or 'bad'. Even when I answered them back and accused them of treating me unfairly, at the back of my mind I thought I must deserve the punishments I received and that there was something wrong with me.

The revelation that I wasn't the only one came one night, when I woke up and heard whispered voices outside my bedroom door. I squeezed my eyes shut and began to pray, 'Please don't let them beat me, God. I'm sure I haven't done anything bad today. Please.' I heard a muffled sound like a door being opened, but when I squinted through my eyelashes, the door to my room was still shut.

I held my breath to listen and then, after a few moments, slipped silently out of bed, tiptoed across the room and, hoping no one else would be able to hear the loud thumping of my heart, turned the handle of the door until it was open just enough for me to be able to see out into the corridor with one eye.

There was no one there and I was just beginning to think I'd dreamed the whole thing when two nuns came out of a bedroom diagonally opposite mine, pulling behind them a girl called Caitlin.

Caitlin was making a strange mewling sound, similar to the one I sometimes made when I was very frightened, and she was begging, 'Please don't hurt me. I'm sorry. I'm sorry.' I don't know what gave me the courage to follow them. I think perhaps it was because I was so shocked by the thought that maybe I wasn't the only 'Devil's child'. Could it be possible that Caitlin was one too? I had to find out.

The nuns took Caitlin to the same room where they usually took me – the one with the bed and the large crucifix on the wall. I stood outside it with my ear pressed against the door and listened. Most of the time, I couldn't hear what the nuns were saying, but I did hear one of them shout, 'You are a disgusting, dirty little girl.' Then I heard a thud, followed quickly by another, and, from the half-swallowed screams, I knew they'd gagged her like they always gagged me and that they were beating her.

There were tears streaming down my face, and when I crept back to my bedroom, I sat on my bed for a long time, crying and rocking backwards and forwards.

The next day, I watched Caitlin from a distance and as soon as she was on her own, I walked up to her and asked if she was okay.

'Yes,' she answered, looking at me with a closed-off, unfriendly expression.

'I know what happened to you last night,' I whispered. 'I was there. I wanted to do something to help you, but I was too scared. I'm sorry.'

She looked at me for just a split-second with an expression of shocked surprise and then her face flushed crimson and she snapped at me, 'Mind your own business,' before glancing round and adding, in a quick, frightened voice, 'I want to stay here with my sister and brother. If I say anything, the nuns will send me away.' She looked directly into my eyes again and then she turned her back on me and walked out of the room.

I followed Caitlin on another night too, when the nuns dragged her to the chapel, where they forced her on to her knees in front of the altar and made her pray aloud that God would make her pure. Afterwards, they left her standing outside in the freezing cold with her hands on her head. But when I tried to talk to her about it the next day, she denied anything had happened and told me I must have been dreaming – although the fear in her eyes told me otherwise.

I was ashamed of the fact that I felt almost glad to have

discovered I wasn't the only one. Although other people's pain has always distressed me, and I know it sounds selfish to say it, the knowledge that the nuns weren't just punishing me made me feel as though I wasn't alone, which I'd always thought I was. And after I found out about Caitlin, I began to look at other children too, when they got into trouble, and to wonder just how many of them were being subjected to the same treatment I had been suffering for so long.

The speech impediment I'd started to develop shortly after the beatings began was getting worse. The problem was that, as well as making it difficult for other people to understand what I was trying to say – which they weren't much inclined to bother doing in the first place – stuttering so badly that I was unable to express myself added to my frustration, which further fuelled the angry bewilderment I already felt and made my behaviour even worse.

Things were becoming more difficult for me at school too, not least because I think I'd decided that if I was going to be called the Devil's child anyway, I might as well stop bothering to try to be good.

So a vicious circle was set in motion: the more beatings I got, the worse my stammer and my behaviour became, and then the more beatings I got. Not every punishment I received was as bad as the ones I've described though; sometimes I just got a clip round the head or was hit with a slipper or the iron spoon. But I don't think a single day passed when I didn't get into trouble for something.

It was the mental as much as the physical abuse that was wearing me down, and before long there was one thing I had in common with the nuns and with some of the other children: the fact that I shared their hatred of *me*. I was an outcast and I knew I was unworthy of anyone's love – although for reasons I wasn't quite clear about. There were many incidents that drove that message home to me and made me aware that I wasn't as good as the other children in any way. For example, sometimes all the other children except me would be given lollipops, and although it hurt and upset me, I learned to accept my exclusion as part of the natural order of things – lollipops were treats or rewards that were given only to those who deserved them.

I'd often listen to other children being praised for something they'd done and my heart would almost burst with longing for someone to say something similar to me. But I was never praised, however hard I tried to be good; instead, all I ever got were snide remarks and criticism that chipped away at my already diminished confidence until I was so demoralised nothing seemed to matter anymore.

When I was punished, I would protest loudly and bitterly about the unfairness of it all. Afterwards though, when I was alone in my bed with my hands crossed over my chest and my eyes wide open, waiting to see if the nuns were going to come for me that night, I'd tell myself angrily, 'It's your own fault, Jerry Coyne. If you hadn't allowed the Devil to get inside you, you wouldn't always be getting yourself into trouble, and the nuns wouldn't always be trying to beat him out of you again.'

I often wondered why the Devil had chosen *me*: surely there were other children whose souls were just as dark as mine? Even within the small world of the children's home, there were other children who got into trouble. So why was I any worse than they were? Why didn't my parents want me and why had my brother and two of my sisters gone to live with our dad and left me and Teresa at Nazareth House?

Most of the time, I didn't know what I was doing wrong – except when the anger built up and I lashed out, using my fists to try to transfer the pain inside me into physical pain for someone else. And because I didn't know what I was doing wrong, I didn't know how to stop doing it.

For example, I remember one dinner time at school when a bowl of pudding was put down on the table in front of me and I said, politely, 'No custard, please.' It seemed a reasonable enough thing to say, because I hated custard; even the smell of it made me retch. But the teacher ignored my request and when I refused to eat the pudding, she tried to force-feed it to me with a spoon.

'I don't want it,' I stammered, turning my head away. 'I hate custard. It makes me sick. I can't eat it.' But she kept pushing the spoon up against my lips until I swung my arm and knocked it out of her hand. She leapt to her feet just as I picked up the bowl of pudding and threw it on the ground, shouting at her, 'I told you. I don't want it!'

The teacher was furious – understandably to some extent, I suppose. Grabbing my ear tightly between her thumb and forefinger, she pulled me to my feet and half pushed, half dragged me to the headmistress's office. She knocked on the door and went into the room, leaving me sitting outside in the corridor, fuming with righteous indignation, and when she came out again a few minutes later, I was called in to see the headmistress.

The lecture I received was pretty much what I'd expected. The headmistress was clearly very angry as she told me that behaviour like mine could not be tolerated, and when I tried to explain to her what had happened, she shouted at me, 'I am absolutely determined not to allow the good name of this school to be dragged through the dirt because of one ungrateful, maladjusted child who doesn't know how to behave in a decent, Christian manner.'

She pushed her chair back, stood up and leant across the desk towards me as she stormed, 'You think you can do whatever you want. But you cannot. You cause nothing but trouble and I will not put up with it for one moment longer.'

Suddenly I felt angry too and I shouted back at her, 'Get rid of me then. Why don't you? You're always saying you're going to, but you never do anything about it.'

At that moment, the door opened and the deputy head teacher took three quick strides across the room towards me and hit the side of my head. Then he dragged me back to the now-empty dining room and tried to force me to eat a bowl of custard – only stopping when I was sick all down the front of his shirt.

The truth was that, despite my defiance and apparent bravado, whenever I felt cornered or threatened, I became very frightened. But because I was determined not to show my fear, I suppressed it until it built up and became a rage that burst out of me like an uncontrollable force, making me feel even more afraid. I often felt cornered, because I was often frustrated and because people always seemed to be trying to make me do things I didn't want to do, for reasons I didn't understand.

For example, when the time came for all the children of my age at school to be confirmed into the Catholic Church, we each had to choose a saint's name as a middle name for ourselves and a few days before the confirmation mass, a nun asked me what name I'd chosen.

'John,' I told her proudly, 'after my brother.'

She looked at me for a moment and then one corner of her mouth lifted into a sneer as she said, 'We've chosen Paul.'

'But I want it to be John,' I stammered. 'I don't want Paul. We were told we could choose our own names and I want John.'

I could feel a tremor building up inside me, like the first rumblings of an earthquake, and by the time I'd finished the sentence, I was stuttering so badly it didn't sound as though I was saying real words at all.

'It's Paul,' the nun snapped at me. 'Now run along and say no more about it.'

The night before my confirmation, I was still insisting I wanted to take my brother's name when, suddenly, Sister Dominic leant down until her face was just inches away from mine and hissed at me like an angry snake, 'Your brother would not want a Devil like you to use his name. You will not be taking the name of John because you are not worthy of it.'

When I answered her back, my punishment was to clean all the other children's shoes, and I was halfway through the task when the door of the room crashed open and she came in. She was holding the iron spoon in her right hand and striking it repeatedly against her left palm as she told me how disappointed she was that I'd shown absolutely no gratitude for the fact that she'd bothered to take the time to choose a confirmation name for me.

She began to rant at me about my general lack of appreciation for anything that was ever done for me, and the third time she waved the spoon in my face, I picked up a shoe in one hand, stood up and backed slowly away from her until I could feel the cool roughness of the wall behind me. And that's when she hit my arm, hard, with the spoon.

With my heart thudding and my hands slippery with sweat, I raised the shoe above my head and stammered, 'I'll do it. I'll hit you. I mean it.'

Sister Dominic looked at me coldly for a moment and then, to my amazement, turned on her heels and walked back towards the door. She paused with her hand on the handle and turned to look at me again as she said, 'Don't think this is the end of the matter.' Then she opened the door and left the room.

I knew immediately I'd made a terrible mistake. By answering her back and threatening her, I'd virtually guaranteed for myself an even harsher punishment than normal. But it was too late to do anything about it. So I finished polishing the shoes and walked along the corridor to the lounge, where the other children were watching television.

Later, when Sister Dominic came into the room to turn off the TV and tell us it was time for bed, I tried to hide amongst a group of taller kids as they left the room. But I was still a few feet away from the door when she said, 'Not you, Jerry Coyne. I want a word with you.'

Some of the other children laughed, and one of them muttered the words 'iron spoon' as he pushed past me on his way to the door.

'Stand in the hallway until I've put the other children to bed,' Sister Dominic told me coldly, pointing to a spot outside the lounge and smiling a small, humourless smile.

It must have been almost an hour later when she came downstairs again and led the way to her office, where she was joined after a few minutes by Sister Mary, who was holding the iron spoon and what looked like a rolling pin.

'I'll show you what happens to evil children when they try to get the better of *me*,' Sister Dominic shouted at me, her face puce with fury. 'I'll teach you to answer me back and to threaten me!' Then she began to hit me with the spoon, and as I tried to avoid the blows, I stumbled and fell.

With my arms raised in an attempt to protect my head from the worst of her assault, I struggled to my feet and made a dash for the door. But Sister Mary was one step ahead of me and she stood in front of it, blocking my one escape route and waving the rolling pin in my face. She hit me with it once, on the side of the head, and again I fell to the floor, although this time, instead of thinking about trying to escape, I rolled my body into a ball and didn't even attempt to fend off their attack.

Afterwards, Sister Dominic told me to go to the chapel and pray while I waited for her to come back and send me to bed. I didn't really know what to say to God, except to tell him that the reason I'd so badly wanted to have my brother's name was because it would have made me feel as though I had some connection to him.

The next day, when I was confirmed, I was given the middle name Paul – the name the nuns had chosen for me. I don't know why I'd tried to resist it; I was never going to win against them. But it seemed I never learned – or maybe it was because I still had just enough spirit left in me to refuse to give up hope.

# Chapter Five

Sometimes, after they'd beaten me, the nuns would give me sweets or chocolate. One of them would hold out her hand, with her fingers still wrapped tightly around whatever treat she was offering me, and say, 'You know, don't you, that you mustn't speak to anyone about the punishment you have just received? Promise me now.' And I'd promise, because I wanted the sweets and because I didn't have anyone to tell anyway.

The sad thing is that children can get used to almost anything, especially when they have no way of knowing what normality is like for other children and therefore that the treatment they're receiving isn't 'normal'. So, eventually, it wasn't so much the beatings themselves that wore me down as the waiting. For example, I might do something wrong on a Monday and not be woken up by a nun standing in the darkness beside my bed until the following weekend, by which time I'd have lain awake night after night in anticipation of the beating I knew was coming, and I'd be exhausted.

I don't know what the point of making me wait was, particularly because by the time they came for me, I'd often forgotten what I was being punished for. Maybe the waiting was all part of the punishment. It was certainly like a torture, because every time I did something bad and a night passed without a beating, and then another, and another, I'd lie in bed and think, *Maybe they've forgotten. Maybe this time they won't come.* But they always did.

One evening, I was told by one of the nuns to go immediately to see Sister Adrian in her office. Unusually, I hadn't been in any kind of trouble at all that day, and as I stood nervously outside the door, racking my brain trying to think what I could have done wrong, the thought struck me that maybe the nuns could read my mind, like God could. It was something I'd worried about before, particularly on the many occasions when I'd thought something bad and a nun had suddenly turned round and glared at me. I began to feel really anxious, because if that *was* the case and they knew the things I sometimes said to them in my head, I was in deep trouble.

I wiped the palms of my hands on my shorts and knocked on the door, and as I stepped into the room, Sister Adrian looked up from her desk and smiled at me.

'I think it's high time we got rid of that stammer of

yours,' she said. 'Shall we kneel down and pray together? You will have to pray very hard for God's help.'

My stammer was like a key that locked the door to the glass-walled room in which I seemed to spend so much of my time. I could see and hear everything that went on around me, but I couldn't join in, because I couldn't say any of the things I wanted to say and, when I tried, the other children either lost patience and didn't wait for me to 'spit it out' or they laughed at me, mimicking my voice. So the thought that the stammer could be 'got rid of' and that the soul-destroying frustration it caused me might come to an end was exciting.

I knelt beside Sister Adrian on the wooden floor, clasped my hands together tightly and prayed until my knees were numb and I could see flashes of light behind my tightly closed eyelids. Then, just as we were standing up again, there was a light knock on the door and Sister Dominic and Sister Mary came into the room.

Sister Adrian opened a Bible, pushed it across the desk towards me and told me to read the part she was pointing to. I was even more nervous than normal, because I associated being in Sister Adrian's office with being in trouble and because the two nuns who seemed to hate me most were standing looking at me with expressions of ill-disguised distaste. But I took a deep breath and began to read.

Jerry Coyne

'A . . . A . . . And th . . . th . . . the L . . . L . . . L . . .'

'Stop it!' Sister Dominic slapped my head as she barked the words at me.

'Read it again,' Sister Adrian said.

I bent my head over the Bible again and touched the first word on the line to try to stop it jumping around on the page. But the harder I tried, the more I stuttered, stammered and sounded like a fool, and the more the nuns slapped my head.

Suddenly, Sister Mary reached out her hand, pushed my head down on to the pages of the Bible and shouted, 'Read it! Just read it!' Then she kicked me and I fell on the floor. Instinctively, I raised my arms and tried to cover my head and, as I did so, I could feel fury flooding through my body. Did they think I stuttered on purpose? Didn't they have any idea how badly I wanted to be able to speak like everyone else, how humiliating it was to try as hard as you possibly could to say something and the only sound that came out of you was a stupid noise no one could understand?

As I lay on the floor, with hot tears of disappointment and self-loathing trickling down my cheeks, Sister Dominic snatched the Bible from the desk and brought it crashing down on my head. Then she hit me with it again and again, until darkness seemed to fill the room.

88

I don't know if the nuns really thought that bullying and frightening me would cure my stammer and make me speak properly. But maybe they finally realised it wasn't going to work because eventually they took me to the chapel, where they left me until bedtime to pray for God's forgiveness and to beg him to take away the stammer that the Devil had inflicted on me. And I did pray, fervently. I knelt on the floor in front of the altar and told God I was sorry. I pleaded with Him to cure my stammer, stop the nuns beating me and, if He possibly could, find someone – anyone at all would do – who would love me.

Nothing changed though, and I was just on the verge of trying to come to terms with the fact that I obviously hadn't prayed in the right way, or maybe hadn't used the right words, when I made friends with a boy at school called Phil Devlin.

I'd noticed Phil smiling at me a few times and he'd shouted, 'Good catch!' after he'd passed me the ball in the playground once. And then, one day, he asked me why none of the teachers seemed to like me.

'It's because I'm the Devil's child,' I told him.

Phil looked shocked. 'But of course you're not the Devil's child,' he said. 'Who told you that?'

'The nuns,' I answered miserably. And then, because he was being nice to me and I thought I should try to show my gratitude, I added, 'It's a good idea not to be my friend. No one likes me. So if you *were* my friend, they wouldn't like you either.'

Phil looked at me with a strange expression on his face, and although I felt a small, virtuous glow because I'd done the 'right thing' by warning him, my overriding feeling was of regret because I knew that, by telling him the truth, I'd just lost the chance of having a friend.

At school the next day, Phil smiled at me as I walked into the classroom. There were a couple of times during the morning when I could have sworn he was trying to catch my eye, and then at break time he came running across the playground calling my name and asked me breathlessly, 'Will you come and stay at my house for the weekend?'

At first, I didn't understand what he meant. Why would the family of a boy like Phil ask a boy like me to stay at their house for even half an hour, let alone a whole weekend? It didn't make sense. I decided it must be a joke and that if I said yes, he'd laugh at me for having been stupid enough to have believed him.

'Why?' I asked him, shrugging my shoulders and trying to hide my confused embarrassment by sounding aggressive. 'Why would you want me to stay with you?'

'Because you're my friend,' Phil said. He raised his eyebrows as though the question was really too daft to need an answer, and then he *did* laugh. But instead of ridiculing me, he put his hand on my shoulder and said, 'Great! So that's settled. You will come, won't you?'

By some miracle, Phil's parents managed to get Mother Superior's approval and at last the day arrived when they were coming to pick me up to take me home with them for a whole weekend. Although there was still a part of me that didn't believe it was really going to happen, I was almost beside myself with excitement. So my heart sank when Mother Superior called me into her office.

I knew she was going to say that Phil's parents had changed their minds. But, to my amazement, she made me look directly into her eyes and told me, sternly, that I was *not* to discuss my life at Nazareth House with the Devlins, or with anyone else. Then she sent me to wait for them by the front door.

As I stood in the hallway, my whole body quivering with anxiety and anticipation, a nun walked past me and whispered, 'They won't like you. No one likes wicked children.' And I knew that she was right.

By the time Phil and his parents arrived, I'd convinced myself that it would be far better not to go with them. I felt sick with disappointment, but I couldn't bear the thought of doing something wrong and of seeing the dislike in their eyes when they looked at me. So I was more than surprised when the nun who answered the door when the bell rang was charm and friendliness personified.

Instead of warning Phil's parents about me, as I'd expected her to do, she patted my shoulder, smiled and told me to be a good boy and have a lovely time. Then – while I stared at her, open-mouthed with astonishment – she waved cheerily and said, 'We'll see you on Sunday.'

Phil's house was in a good part of town and everyone in his family was really nice. When we all sat at the dining table together to eat our lunch, his parents asked me questions about myself and about what I liked doing – just as I'd always imagined the parents of the real family I sometimes dreamed about being part of would do. After lunch, Phil and I rode bicycles and played football together, and he never left my side for the whole weekend. They were the best two days of my entire life.

When Sunday evening came and it was time to go back to Nazareth House, I had to clench my fists very hard to stop myself crying. Phil's mum gave me the biggest hug I'd ever had, told me it had been 'absolutely lovely' having me to stay and said she hoped I'd come back again very soon. In my head, I was screaming, 'Don't make me leave. Please don't send me back.' But I managed to tell her politely that I'd really, really like that and I'd had a great time.

When I got back to Nazareth House, Mother Superior asked me if I'd managed to behave myself and not bring terrible disgrace on her and all the nuns who cared for

me and were so good to me. I told her I'd been so good
that Mrs Devlin had asked me to go to stay with them
again. But she didn't seem to be listening to what I said,
and instead of congratulating or praising me, she told me
to 'hurry along now' and go to the chapel to pray.

It was dark and cold in the chapel. I knelt on the stone
floor in front of the altar, looked up at Jesus on the cross
and thought about the Devlins, about the weekend I'd
just spent with them and about the fact that Phil's life
was so different from mine it was as though we were living
in completely separate, parallel worlds.

After what seemed like hours, when my knees were
aching and red with cold, a nun came and told me to go
to bed. 'We forgot you were here,' she said, shrugging her
shoulders and laughing. When I looked at the clock, it was
twenty minutes past nine, which meant I'd missed both
tea and supper and that all the other children would already
be in bed. But I didn't care. I'd had a weekend that had
been better than any weekend I'd ever imagined it was
possible for a child to have.

At school the next day, Phil was anxious to know
whether I'd enjoyed staying with his family and if I'd want
to do it again. I told him I had and I would, but I decided
it was probably best not to add the thought that was going
through my head, which was that, given half a chance, I'd
have packed a bag and moved in with them that very day.

I did go to the Devlins' house again, several times over the next few months, and they were always just as kind to me as they had been on that first occasion. During my visits to them, they took me camping and included me in all their weekend activities. But I doubt whether Phil ever really understood what his friendship meant to me or how his family's kindness was the one solitary light that had ever shone in the otherwise almost completely unremitting darkness of my childhood.

When Mrs Devlin gave birth to a baby that was very ill, it was heartbreaking for all the family, and it meant that my visits had to stop. I understand the reason now, of course, but at the time it felt like yet another rejection and, as a result, my behaviour once again became explosive and disruptive as I struggled – and failed – to cope with my disappointment.

In fact, I do have a few other good memories of my childhood, such as the two weeks in the summer when all the children from Nazareth House were taken to stay in a guesthouse by the coast. There was a buzz of excitement for days before our departure, and when the Saturday morning finally arrived, we were all packed and ready to go long before the bus was due at ten o'clock. Several children waited on the driveway, jostling and pushing each other, all wanting to be the first to see the bus arrive, and even the nuns were less brusque than usual as they tried to keep control of the excitement that was bubbling out of all of us.

When we arrived at our destination – a huge white house just yards from the sea – we were greeted by Bob, who ran the guesthouse with his wife, Dora. Nothing was too much trouble for Bob and Dora, and it was thanks to them – and to their extraordinary ability to cope, calmly and patiently, with a house full of screaming, over-excited children – that we had a holiday of a lifetime.

We slept two, three or four to a double bed, lying top to toe with our noses just inches from the seaweed smell of the feet of the child lying next to us. And if it hadn't been for the fact that we spent each day running around in the sun and breathing in so much fresh sea air that we were totally exhausted, I think we'd have stayed awake all night talking and wouldn't have slept at all.

Bob was one of the kindest, friendliest people I've ever met. He had a little café attached to the guesthouse and when everyone else was occupied I'd sometimes sneak back there and he'd give me an ice cream, raising his finger to his lips and whispering to me that I mustn't tell the other children or he'd have no ice cream left to sell to his customers.

Every day was sunny, and as soon as we'd eaten our breakfast, we'd run down to the beach, where we'd spend hours darting in and out of the sea, playing beach ball, hunting for crabs and building sandcastles. In the late afternoon, we'd walk back to the guesthouse for a huge tea, cooked by Bob, after which we'd be given some money and taken to the fair.

Those two weeks couldn't have been more different from my normal, everyday life. We were given a freedom on that holiday that I'd never previously experienced. It was as if I'd been told to think of all the things I'd love to do and was being allowed to do them. Even the nuns were nice to me – or, at least, they weren't 'not nice'. But one of the best moments of every day was when we all met up at nine o'clock in the evening, after having been to the fair, and walked back to the guesthouse together, eating bags of chips and singing at the tops of our voices. Because it was in those moments that I felt as though I was part of something, which was the one thing I'd always longed to be.

It seemed that those two weeks in the summer were the only time the nuns relaxed too. In the normal course of life at Nazareth House, I don't remember any of them ever giving any sign that they were happy or even mildly contented, and I often wondered how many of them had actually wanted to be nuns. But I suppose sleeping for just four hours a night, as they usually did, is probably enough to make anyone bad-tempered – although even persistent sleep deprivation doesn't cause most people to become cruel and brutal. And I should know, because my sleep has been interrupted by nightmares for as long as I can remember.

Sadly though, we hadn't been driving for long on our way back to Nottingham at the end of our holiday before the nuns began to look sour and irritable again, and I knew that by the time we reached Nazareth House, everything would have returned to being the way it normally was.

And it wasn't long before my behaviour was back to 'normal' too. In fact, it began to get worse. Although Phil Devlin had explained to me that his baby brother's illness was the only reason I couldn't spend weekends with his family anymore, I was convinced they'd turned against me because they'd decided I wasn't such a nice boy after all. It was a crushing disappointment and I felt as though I'd been rejected once again.

My speech impediment was so bad by that time that I'd sometimes stutter for so long no one was prepared to wait to find out what I wanted to say – and they often couldn't understand me even when I did manage to say it. As my stammer got worse, I became more belligerent. I was already an angry child, and the embarrassment of not being able to make myself understood increased my frustration to the point at which I'd lash out and punch anyone who upset me or got in my way.

My teachers had lost any control of me they'd ever had, and I knew it. The three words I *could* say with the minimum degree of stuttering were 'no' and 'fuck off'. I resented the children who wore nice clothes and went home to nice houses with their nice parents every day. I would watch them arriving at school in the mornings – being kissed and hugged by their mums and dads – and again when they were picked up while I was waiting for the bus to take me back to Nazareth House at the end of every afternoon. It was like scratching at a scab until the wound opened and bled again. But I couldn't help myself.

I got into a fight with two older boys one day, when one of them told me, 'You must be a bastard if you've got no mum and dad.' They were both much bigger than me, and much stronger, and despite the anger that often gave me the edge in a fight, they thrashed me. But because it was important to me not to be seen to be hurt or upset, I pretended not to care, and as they walked away, I wiped the blood from my face with the back of my hand and called after them, 'I'll get you, both of you. Just you wait and see. You better watch your backs.'

It must have sounded like a pathetically empty threat from a small boy with a bloody nose and a busted lip, and one of them flashed a V sign over his shoulder without even bothering to turn around. Clearly, though, they hadn't understood the power of the anger inside me.

The next day, I spotted one of the boys clambering over a fence opposite the school. I waited for him to drop down into a field on the other side and then I followed him. By the time I caught up with him, he was standing with his back to me, throwing stones at some cows and laughing when they bumped and butted each other as they tried to get away.

He didn't hear me approaching, so he was taken completely by surprise when I jumped on his back and started punching his head, and when he fell on the ground, I shoved his face into a cow pat and shouted, 'And that's for hurting the cows.'

The next day, his mate came up to me in the playground and tried to make friends by offering to give me a bag of marbles and some money. But it was too late. The two boys had become the physical embodiment of all the things that had hurt me in my life and I couldn't control the anger inside me. I snatched his bag of marbles out of his hands and sent them rolling and skittering across the playground, and then I punched him on the nose – at exactly the moment when the deputy head teacher walked out of the school building. A few seconds later, I was being held by the ear and marched off to the deputy head's office, where I was given the thrashing that – on that occasion – I probably deserved.

Apart from my defiance and bad behaviour, another

thing about me that both the nuns and my teachers found unacceptable was the fact that I was left-handed. They called it 'wrong-handedness' and they seemed to think that, like my stammer, it was wilful contrariness on my part. The nuns often shook their heads and told me, 'It's the sign of having been touched by the Devil.' And I believed them. So I was almost as anxious to learn to use my right hand as they were to force me to do so. But no matter how hard I tried, I just couldn't do things right-handed and, as a result, I fell even further behind in my education until, eventually, my teachers simply stopped bothering to try to teach me anything at all.

Everyone gave up on me. In their eyes, I was obstinately determined to continue stuttering and stammering so badly I couldn't make myself understood, I refused to write with the 'correct' hand, and my behaviour was bad – for no good reason that anyone could possibly think of. And, I suppose, if you looked only at the effect and not the cause, who wouldn't be tempted to give up on that child?

Finally though, the nuns did get me to use my knife and fork in the 'correct' hands. It was a feat they accomplished by means of determination and resolve – and by bashing my elbows on the table every time I made a mistake. Otherwise, I was left to spend my days playing with the school's pet hamsters in the corner of the classroom or sitting outside the headmistress's office waiting to be held to account for my latest exploit – which was usually rudeness to a teacher or an apparently unwarranted and unprovoked attack on a fellow pupil.

And then, one day, completely out of the blue, one of the nuns told me that I was going to go to my dad's for the weekend. At first I couldn't believe it. I thought the nun was just being mean – winding me up and getting me all excited so she could laugh and say again what they were always telling me: 'No one wants you, Jerry Coyne.' But, to my amazement, it turned out to be true.

In fact, I didn't really care much about seeing my dad – I couldn't forgive him for putting us in a children's home in the first place and then for leaving me and Teresa there when he took the others to live with him. But I was very excited about the prospect of seeing John, Geraldine and Carmella. Ever since the day they'd gone to live with our dad in a real house, I'd envied my brother and sisters – although I soon changed my mind when I saw for myself how they were actually living.

The house was bleak, cold and horrible. There were no carpets on the floors upstairs, just rough, splintered floorboards; all the walls were bare, unpainted plaster; and although the living room was warm, the rest of the house was freezing. It didn't seem to matter how many clothes you wore in bed, you were still so cold that it was difficult to get to sleep. Dad's bedroom had a padlock on the door. I never saw inside it and I used to wonder what he was hiding in there – although perhaps it was best not to know! Worst of all though – worse than the biting cold and the austere drabness of the house – was the way Dad treated us, which was the way he'd been treating the others all the time I'd been imagining them gathered together around the dining table, rosy cheeked and cheerful, eating good food and talking to each other like I'd seen the Devlins do.

I was shocked by the reality of the lives my brother and sisters were leading. In those days, pubs opened for four hours over lunchtime and then from seven till ten thirty in the evening, and when he wasn't working, Dad was in the local pub with his mates for as many of those hours as possible. At weekends, he'd often sleep on the couch in the afternoons, but it was as though he had some sort of internal alarm clock and he never failed to wake up at five minutes to seven, just in time to go back out to the pub again.

On the first weekend when Teresa and I went home, the nuns had given us some pocket money, which we gave to Geraldine, and while Dad was out on the Saturday evening, we all went to a late-night café down the road and played pinball. Then we spent the rest of the money on a huge bag of chips, which we ate as we hurried through the streets to get home before the pubs shut, so that Dad wouldn't discover we'd been out.

The only time we could ever relax was when Dad was at the bookies or the pub, although even then he'd sometimes sneak back silently to see what we were up to. So it was lucky he never caught John robbing the gas meter. It took ages to slide a knife in through the slit in the meter and 'liberate' a few 5p pieces. But John was very patient and he eventually perfected a technique, although he always held his breath when the man came to empty the meter, because he knew he'd get a thrashing from Dad if he got found out. Perhaps the meter man didn't care one way or the other, though, because he never said anything, which meant that when the nuns didn't give Teresa and me any pocket money, we often still had enough to play pinball and buy a bag of chips when Dad was at the pub.

Dad ruled all of us through fear, and even on that first weekend I could almost see the tension in my brother and sisters. I went home for a few weekends after that, and I can remember exactly how it felt to sit huddled together in silence waiting for Dad to return from the pub and to find out what sort of mood he was in. It seemed as though we'd been set free when he sent us to bed, particularly for me, because the one good thing about being there was that I knew no nuns were going to appear beside me in the night and drag me out of my bed for a beating – except, of course, in my nightmares.

John and my sisters were only allowed to have one bath a week, at the weekend, and when I was there, I had to have one too. Geraldine used to boil up pans of water and pour them into the bathtub for us all to wash in, one by one – girls first, then John and then finally, when the water was grey and cold, me. It wasn't the greatest way to get clean, so I was grateful to John on the occasions when he took me with him to have a bath at his friend Arthur's place instead.

Arthur lived in a warm, comfortable flat with a seem-ingly endless supply of hot water (there was no hot water in any of the taps in Dad's house), and he was a very kind man. Although I think he knew how our father treated us, he never said a word against him; he just did whatever he could to help us, which included letting John and me have hot baths and then cooking us a huge meal, followed by the biggest mug of tea I'd ever seen. He was a much better father figure to John than our own father was, and he provided him with somewhere to escape to when he needed it.

Every weekend I spent at Dad's house, each day started with him shouting at us all to wake up and come down for breakfast – which, like every other meal time, was always scary. He'd call us into the kitchen one by one to pick up a plate of food and a mug of tea, and then we'd walk, very carefully, to the living room while he shouted after us, 'Don't spill it! Watch where you're fucking going!' I was so nervous and my hands used to shake so much that I always slopped tea all over the floor and arrived in the living room with my mug less than half full.

Geraldine was still our 'mum' and the peacemaker of the family. There were many occasions when she jumped in to try to stop Dad hitting one of us – and ended up taking the slaps herself. But she never complained. I was very frightened of my father, and I'd often sit on Geraldine's knee when he was in the house. It was the only place I felt safe, and I always tried to stay close to her until the pubs re-opened and Dad went out again.

It seemed that Carmella hadn't changed much either. She still spoke out for what she thought was right and would often stand toe to toe with Dad while arguing her case – and then take a beating for her convictions. However, John's way of dealing with things was almost the opposite: he'd just stand there with a blank expression on his face while Dad shouted at, bullied and belittled him, and you'd get the feeling he was thinking, 'Rant at me all you want. It doesn't matter, because I know that my day will come.'

But although Dad was very much the master in his

own house, he still bowed to the conventions of the time with regard to being 'a good Catholic'. Every Sunday morning when I was there, he shouted at us as usual to 'get out of fucking bed' and then, after we'd hastily eaten our breakfast, he'd stand by the front door, already dressed in his suit, while we ran around in a panic putting on our clothes.

It would have taken a normal person about fifteen minutes to walk from our house to St Patrick's Church, but it took us less than five to almost run there, with Dad marching behind us, issuing orders like a sergeant major. By the time we got to the church, there'd be several other Irish families queuing up outside the door, all of them eager to show the priest and their neighbours that they were decent, God-fearing Catholics – for an hour or so on Sundays, at least. Because if you didn't go to church every Sunday, the priest would call at your house to find out why – and that was a shameful public indignity no one wanted to risk, including Dad.

So he dragged his children to mass every Sunday without fail, although, once inside the church, he never said a prayer or sang a hymn. He just sat or stood silently, with his shoulders back and his eyes fixed on the window ahead of him, until the service was over. Then we all filed out again and stood on the path in front of the church's porch just long enough for the priest to see we were there, before marching home again, to arrive just in time for Dad to go out to the pub to meet his mates.

As soon as the front door closed behind him, we all released the breath we'd been holding and got out the Monopoly board. We called it 'the fighting game', because I don't think we ever managed to get to the end of a single game without Carmella and John falling out and starting to fight. It was fun though, playing a board game with my own brother and sisters, just like any normal boy in any normal family might do.

I knew right from the start that Dad didn't want me at home, even for the occasional weekend. It was clear he had no interest in me; he rarely spoke to me at all, except to shout at me about something. But although my visits were unwelcome and inconvenient, at least they enabled him to get more money from social security to spend at the pub or on the horses – which is where his real interest lay.

Sometimes the Catholic Children's Society – which was responsible for the care I received – would arrange meetings to talk about my future. Dad never went to them though – until they threatened to send me to live with him full time, and then he was there like a shot, dressed in his suit and expressing a deep concern about my welfare I think everyone knew he didn't have. He told the priest he *really* wanted me to live with him, but, unfortunately, he had high blood pressure and so wouldn't be able to cope with me, particularly in view of my severe behavioural problems.

That was one of the few occasions when he openly acknowledged that there was something wrong with my behaviour. Normally, he tried to make light of it to other people, and would shrug his shoulders and tell my social worker he was sure I'd 'grow out of it'. And, like everyone else it seems, he never bothered to wonder *why* I behaved badly and was so full of anger – I suppose because, also like everyone else, he simply didn't care.

However, my father's determination not to have me living with him didn't matter to me – at least, not on any practical level – because I knew that, were I to leave Nazareth House and go home, it would be very much a case of 'out of the frying pan and into the fire'. On the plus side, it would have meant living with John and my sisters and having Geraldine there to mother and try to protect me, as well as no more beatings from the nuns. On the down side, though, was the fact that I'd be living in his miserable, cold house – at least there were clean rooms and good food at Nazareth House – and waiting in fear for him to get home from the pub every night, not to mention being thrashed whenever he was in a bad mood, which was almost all the time when he was at home.

So I told myself I didn't care that my father didn't want me. I didn't like him anyway. The truth was, though, that it was yet another rejection, and further confirmation of what the nuns were always telling me: nobody wanted me and nobody loved me, not even my own father.

# Chapter Six

The trouble was that because the nuns' dislike of me was an open secret, everyone else took their cue from that fact and it was always open season on teasing and bullying me, so I was constantly getting into scuffles.

We were eating our dinner one day when I got into an argument with another boy and he scratched my face. There was so much negative emotion inside me all the time that it only needed some small incident like that to top it up just enough for it to erupt, and I picked up a chair and slammed it over his head. There was blood everywhere and I was immediately shocked by what I'd done. I was frightened too, because I knew I'd get a beating when the nuns got hold of me. So, while everyone was still screaming and running around like headless chickens, I darted out of the dining room and hid for a few hours, until the worst of the fuss had died down.

I had to come out of hiding some time though, and

when I did, Sister Mary was waiting for me. Dragging me around by the hair seemed to be the sport of choice for several of the nuns when they were really angry, and Sister Mary was no exception. She pulled me into the laundry room and beat me across the head with what felt like a hairbrush. I was dancing around and trying to protect my head with my arms, and although she still had the fingers of one hand entwined in my hair, she managed to make sure that most of her blows met their target and she kept hitting me until I was dizzy.

I was crouching on the floor against the wall when she finally stopped assaulting me and shouted, 'You are an evil boy who does not deserve the care that you are given.' Then she locked me in the laundry room, leaving me to wonder just what 'care' she might have meant.

When it was my bedtime and she came back and unlocked the door, I knew my punishment wasn't over. In bed that night, I tried to stay awake so that I'd hear them coming, but I woke up with a start when Sister Mary prodded my shoulder with her finger and said sharply, 'Come with me.' There were at least two other nuns waiting outside the bedroom door and they walked behind me as I followed Sister Mary down the corridor. Maybe it was because I knew I deserved the punishment I was about to get that I was even more frightened than usual, and by the time we reached the old people's part of the building, the legs of my pyjamas were soaked in urine.

Sister Mary led the way to a bathroom, where it felt as though a dozen hands were reaching out to lift me off the ground by my ankles and wrists. Already shivering with fear, I was thrown into a bath half full of icy-cold water, the shock of which seemed to freeze my lungs so that I couldn't breathe. I still hadn't managed to catch my breath when I felt a strong hand on the back of my head, pushing my body down below the surface of the water. I struggled, kicking out with my legs in panic, and just as I thought I really was going to die, the pressure on my head was released and I shot up out of the water again, coughing and choking and trying to suck air into my lungs.

I was still spluttering and wheezing when I was pushed down for a second time, and at exactly the same moment I felt a sharp blow on my back as one of the nuns hit me with what felt like a wooden coat hanger. It was as if that first blow acted as a signal to all the other nuns, and while Sister Mary repeated the cycle of pushing me under the water and holding me there until I was about to pass out before pulling me up for just long enough to take a few breaths, the other nuns hit me on my back and arms.

My chest ached and I was sobbing and gasping for air

by the time they stopped. Sister Mary began to rant at me, but I couldn't make out what she was saying, because I'd really thought they were going to let me die that time, and I was almost hysterical with terror. She was still hissing venom at me when I was pulled out of the bath. One of the nuns ripped off my pyjamas, threw a towel at me and snapped, 'Dry yourself, Devil's child.' Then all the nuns laughed and jeered at me and reached out their hands to pinch my cold, trembling body.

As I got a bit older, there was talk about sending me to a boarding school, but after the nuns and the headmistress of St Patrick's had written their reports about my abilities and my behaviour, I doubt whether there was a school in the country that would have been willing to take me. My father insisted that I must go to a Catholic school – which was odd, when you take into account the fact that he had absolutely no interest in either my education or my welfare. I had a social worker who was supposed to be responsible for those and all the other things a normal parent might be expected to care about, and she was determined to find a school for me. But when she came to see me one day to tell me that if my behaviour didn't improve, no school was ever going to accept me, she seemed to have lost some of her original resolve.

I told her that I didn't mean to behave badly and I tried

to explain about the nuns and about how they often woke me up in the middle of night to beat me. But talking about the nuns made my stutter worse than ever and I suppose it wasn't really surprising that she didn't seem to be listening to me.

When she interrupted me and said I should be grateful to the nuns and to everyone at Nazareth House for the way they looked after me, I gave in to the frustration and shouted at her that I wanted another social worker, and she stood up, picked up her bag and walked out of the room. I followed her out to her car and as she opened the door to get into it, I managed to say, more calmly this time, 'When are you going to listen to me? I'm telling you the truth. It's the nuns who are lying. They're beating me and telling everyone I'm behaving badly. You're supposed to be on *my* side, but you just ignore what I'm saying and tell me I should be grateful.'

She looked up at me through the open window of her car and sighed as she told me, 'I'm trying to help you, Jerry.' Then she shook her head slowly a couple of times and drove away.

When she left, I felt even more discouraged and miserable than I had before she came. In reality, it wasn't often that I did anything really bad, like punching someone or getting into a fight. But it seemed that even the smallest, most childish thing I did wrong was blown out of all proportion and, as a consequence, I'd become an outsider and an outcast.

I don't remember many occasions when I really relaxed and had fun when I was a child. There weren't many things to look forward to, although I do remember one Christmas morning when we all ran down into the lounge and the Christmas tree was almost surrounded by sacks of toys. In all the Christmases I'd spent at Nazareth House – which were all the Christmases of my life – I had never seen anything like it. I stood and watched as first one child and then another and then another shrieked with excitement as they found a sack with their name on it. Before long, all the girls were screaming and all the boys were whooping with delight as they opened their sacks and began to pull out toys.

I hung back though. I didn't join the other children who were running from sack to sack looking for their names because I didn't think there would be one for me and I wanted to put off the moment when that doubt became a certainty. Eventually, however, when every child seemed to have a sack of toys, there was still one left, standing, unopened, beside the Christmas tree.

Not daring to hope, I edged towards it and, glancing sideways, read the name on the tag: Jerry Coyne. I looked at it again, and then, before anyone had the chance to say, 'That isn't yours, Jerry; we made a mistake,' I almost threw myself on top of it and started to pull out one toy after another. The Christmas presents we were used to getting were a selection box, some fruit and a couple of cheap toys – which were often inappropriate for our gender and/or age. So I could hardly believe my eyes when I saw all the amazing toys that were now lined up on the floor in front of me – and still no one came bustling into the room to snatch them away.

It was an incredible Christmas. The staff served us a wonderful Christmas dinner and even the nuns – who were usually so stone-faced – were cheerful. After dinner, when we were already full to bursting, we all ate too much chocolate and played with our toys until the nuns told us to pack up our sacks. Then we carried them up to our bedrooms and I placed mine just under my bed, where I could reach out my arm to touch it before I went to sleep, to reassure myself that the whole day hadn't been an extraordinary dream.

I was sharing a bedroom with three other boys at that time, and when Sister Mary came in to turn off our light, some of her usual sternness had returned and she said, 'Be quiet now and go to sleep.' But we were far too excited to sleep, and we were still whispering to each other when the door was flung open, the light snapped on again and Sister Mary stormed back into the room shouting, 'I warned you, Jerry Coyne. You were given the same gifts as the other boys, although God knows you've done nothing to deserve them. And this is how you repay the goodness that has been shown to you.'

'B . . . B . . . But it wasn't j . . . j . . . just m . . . me, Sister,' I stammered.

'Of course it was you,' she snapped. 'You're the one who's keeping the other boys awake with your talking.' As she spoke, she bent down, pulled the sack of toys out from underneath my bed and took it with her when she turned off the light, slammed the door and left the room.

'You'll get them back in the morning,' one of the other boys whispered. 'Don't worry now, Jerry. She's just trying to teach you a lesson.'

The next morning, although I was still incensed by the unfairness of what Sister Mary had done, I decided that getting my toys back was infinitely more important to me than trying to make her see that she'd been unjust. So, for once, I managed not to be cheeky or to show my resentment as I told her I was sorry for talking when I should have been going to sleep and asked if I could have my toys. But she just sniffed and said, 'When you deserve them.' Then she turned her back on me and walked away.

I never did seem to deserve them though, so I didn't get them back, and a few days later, when Sister Mary was getting ready to go to visit her family, I was playing in the yard when I saw her put a suitcase and a sack down on the ground beside the minibus that was waiting to take her to the railway station. She didn't see me – either then or when she turned to go back into the building – and as soon as she'd disappeared from sight, I ran over to the minibus and pulled open the sack. I was still staring at the toys inside it when I felt a hand on my shoulder.

Managing to wriggle out of Sister Mary's vice-like grip, I shouted at her, 'Those are *my* toys. What are you doing with them?' But she just looked at me coldly and said, 'You have had every chance to earn them back. But all you ever do is cause trouble. You don't deserve to be given presents. I'm going to throw them away.'

I knew I hadn't done anything wrong. I'd barely been in trouble at all since Christmas, and the only times I *had* been were for minor, silly things that certainly didn't warrant the loss of my Christmas presents.

I knew Sister Mary's brother had a son of about my age and I couldn't help wondering if she was taking my toys to give to him. But even if that were true, there was nothing I could do about it except watch the minibus drive away and shout after it, 'I hate you. You're the one who's evil.'

I ran back to the yard, snatched a football out of the hands of another boy and kicked it against a wall of the building. Then I kicked it again and again, as hard as I could. I was aiming for a window, but missing every time, and slowly my anger became fury and I bent down, picked up the ball and threw it with all my might so that the glass smashed into a thousand pieces.

Within seconds, I'd been summoned to Sister Dominic's office.

'I saw you break that window with my own eyes, Jerry Coyne,' she told me. 'It was a deliberate, mindless act of violence. You are an evil little boy, and you will not receive any pocket money until every single penny of the repair has been paid for.' Then she beat me with the iron spoon until it felt as though every bone in my body was bruised and aching.

I knew it was pointless to try to explain why I'd done it. But when Sister Dominic finally stopped hitting me, I told her anyway – about how Sister Mary had taken my sack of presents as a punishment on Christmas night when I hadn't even been the one talking, how I'd just seen her loading them into the minibus, and how I was certain that she was going to give them to her nephew so that I'd never be able to earn them back like she'd said I could.

I expected Sister Dominic to beat me again for having the impudence to answer back. So I was amazed when she said, 'I'll talk to Sister Mary and you will get your presents back if you promise to behave and keep out of trouble.'

I promised, of course, and when I went to bed that

night, I prayed and prayed to God to make me good so that Sister Mary would have to give my presents back. But even though I crossed my arms over my chest, the Devil must have got inside me somehow, because when Sister Mary returned to Nazareth House, I didn't keep out of trouble as I'd promised, and when I saw her in the dining room, I told her angrily, 'I know what you've done with my presents and I won't ever forgive you.'

'I threw them away,' she told me. And when I shouted, 'You're a liar,' she slapped my face.

She sneered at me and her voice was full of disgust as she asked, 'And what did your father buy you for Christmas? What wonderful present did your mother get for you?'

I stared at her, willing myself not to shed the tears I could feel pricking my eyes and wishing I had an answer to her questions.

'Yes, that's right,' Sister Mary said nastily. 'Nothing. No one else bought you any presents at all. And why do you think that was? I'll tell you why, Jerry Coyne: because no one loves you and no one wants you.'

I turned away from her mean, taunting expression, picked up a chair and hurled it across the room, shouting as I did so, 'You're a fucking liar. I hate you. You can keep your fucking presents. I don't want anything from any of you.' Then I overturned a table and started to pick up anything I could lay my hands on and throw it against the wall.

I'm sure I was punished severely for that particular episode of bad behaviour. But I can't remember how.

I can't remember when I first started sleepwalking either, although I know it wasn't long before I was doing it almost every night. One night, I woke up to find myself in the room the nuns usually took me to for night-time beatings. It was dark, except for the diffused light from the moon that was almost directly in line with the window, and I was standing in front of the crucifix with my hands clasped, as if in prayer.

Waking up anywhere other than in my own bed was always horrible. I'd be frightened and disorientated and it would take me a few seconds to work out where I was. This time though, it was even worse than usual, and as I looked across the room at the bed where the nuns often tied me, I could actually feel the blows raining down on my body. I began to gasp for air and the next thing I knew, I was crouching in the corner of the room with my knees clasped to my chest, sobbing and terrified.

The one thought in my mind was to get out of there as quickly as possible – before one of the nuns came in and I got a real beating. But when I tried to stand up, my legs simply wouldn't obey the command that was being sent to them by my brain, and it seemed like eternity before I finally managed to get on my feet and tiptoe back to my bedroom.

I didn't know then what a flashback is, but I think that was probably the first of the many that continued into my adult life.

I returned to that same room another night, but when I woke up on that occasion, I was huddled on the floor against the wall, in a pool of my own urine. I was sweating and my heart was thumping, and as I looked around me, I could see that everything in the room had been turned upside down. The grey woollen blanket that usually lay across the bed was on the floor near the door, the mattress was hanging off the side of the bed-frame, and – most terrible of all – the crucifix that normally looked down from the wall was lying on the floor next to me.

I could hear a pathetic whimpering sound, and it was a few seconds before I realised it was coming from me. I clutched my knees more tightly against my chest and looked again at the crucifix. And then it seemed as if my heart stopped beating. Where was Jesus? Sobbing, I began to crawl across the floor, searching for the silver figure that should have been attached to the cross, and that's when I became aware that I was gripping something tightly in my left hand. Slowly, I uncurled my fingers and looked down into the face of Christ. With a cry, I hurled the figure across the room and then immediately leapt to my feet to scurry after it.

I was still whimpering as I tidied the room and tried my best to return order to the chaos I'd created. But there was nothing I could do to fix Jesus back on to His cross. So I placed them both carefully on the floor, just underneath the spot on the wall where they usually hung, and then I ran as quickly and silently as I could back to my bedroom, pulled the bedcovers over my head and prayed that no one would ever find out what I'd done.

Another night, I woke up to find myself sitting in a pew at the back of the chapel. It must have been the early hours of the morning, because the nuns were already praying beside the altar, and it was bitterly cold. Very carefully, I slid my bottom forward on the wooden seat and hunched my shoulders in the hope that it would make me less conspicuous while I tried to think what to do. The palms of my hands were damp with sweat and I had to concentrate hard to make myself breathe in and out slowly through my nose so that the panic didn't overwhelm me.

After a moment, I decided that no one would notice me if I slipped out quietly through the main door of the chapel while the nuns were praying. But just as I put one cold, bare foot down on the floor of the aisle, a heavy hand fell on my shoulder and Sister Dominic hissed at me, 'What are you doing here at this time of night?'

My mind was racing as I searched for a credible answer, and then, with a flash of inspiration, I whispered, 'I woke up and couldn't get back to sleep, Sister. So I came here to pray. I'm trying to be good.'

I looked at her as I spoke, and I could see from the expression on her face that she didn't believe me. In the absence of any other, more plausible, explanation, however, she had no choice but to release her grip on my shoulder and watch me with narrowed eyes as I tiptoed towards the door and out of the chapel.

There were many other nights when I woke up in the vestry, a bathroom, the old people's sitting room or the dining room – where, on one occasion, I released the budgie from his cage while I was still asleep and spent almost an hour trying to catch him again when I woke up. Worst of all, though, was the time I found myself standing in a field. I could feel something hot and heavy pushing down on my left shoulder and my nostrils were full of a foul, putrid stench I didn't recognise. Still half asleep, I screamed, and whatever it was also made a loud, blood-curdling noise and then hit me hard on the side of my head so that I fell in a terrified, quivering heap on to the muddy ground.

When the world stopped spinning and I dared to open

my eyes, Mickey, Nazareth House's resident donkey, was glaring down at me with his braying lips so close to my face that the smell of his breath almost made me pass out.

It was when my sleepwalking was at its height that I was sent to see a whole series of doctors, psychologists and therapists. Looking back on it now, it doesn't take a genius to work out what was wrong with me. But without the benefit of knowing the truth about how I was being treated, the consensus seemed to be that I was 'maladjusted'. I think that means I couldn't deal with relationships and with the stresses of daily life. So it was a diagnosis that, had I understood it at the time, I'd have had no reason to argue with. In fact, it was spot on, although the 'daily life' I was trying to adjust to – with such a notable lack of success – was being beaten regularly by the nuns and told that no one loved me or cared about me because I was the wicked spawn of the Devil.

When I did manage to pluck up the courage to try to tell one of the doctors what was happening, he asked me a lot of questions about the nuns and about my life at Nazareth House, which he repeated when I saw him again on another occasion. But he didn't do anything – or, at least, nothing that filtered through to me and made any difference to my life.

Another specialist didn't ask me any questions at all. He just gave me some toys to play with and I sat in his office while he made phone calls and rifled through the bits of paper on his desk, glancing up at me from time to time only to tell me to play more quietly because he was trying to work.

I was a problem to everyone, and eventually the Catholic Children's Society came up with a plan to 'advertise' me in the local church's newsletters to try to find a foster family willing to take me on. I was excited when my social worker told me about it. It was what I'd always wanted – to live with a family – and as I waited for news, I often sat on my bed hugging my knees to my chest and trying to imagine what my new life was going to be like.

They did have one or two enquiries – which is amazing when you consider that they wrote in the 'advertisement': 'This boy has many behavioural problems.' And I imagine that when anyone did show any interest, they read out to them the long list of what those 'behavioural problems' actually were and were then left saying into an echoing phone, 'Hello? Are you still there? Hello?'

So, like so many other things in my young life, it all proved to be a huge disappointment and waste of time. In fact, it's very surprising that, at the age of eleven, I still had any optimism left in me at all. I suppose that whatever happens to young children, they remain naïve enough to keep hoping.

In reality, though, the impact of that experience was far

more devastating than I ever let on. Of course, I realise now that my social worker *had* to tell people 'the truth' as she knew it. But I didn't know at the time why no one wanted to foster me, and it seemed to be yet more proof that what the nuns had always told me was true and, quite literally, no one wanted me, not even gift-wrapped and accompanied by reasonably generous financial compensation for their time and trouble.

I did try to be good. I used to spend hours in the old people's part of the house, helping with the cleaning and listening to their stories – although that was actually something I enjoyed doing, so perhaps it doesn't really count. For a while, I even turned nark, trying to curry favour by reporting to the nuns what other kids did wrong. But nothing made any difference.

The one useful thing I did learn while I was at Nazareth House was to be polite. We were never given a second chance: if you didn't say 'please' when you asked for something, you didn't get it; and if you didn't say 'thank you' when it was given to you, it was snatched away again. In fact, I'm still one of the politest – albeit psychologically scarred – people you're ever likely to meet!

Clearly, it wasn't just me who was suffering as a result of what was supposed to be a good Catholic upbringing. Angela Allen, a woman who is currently serving an indeterminate prison sentence for her part in an online paedophile ring, was a child at Nazareth House when I was there. According to the newspapers, she was described by detectives as 'sinister and evil' and by a doctor as 'emotionally vulnerable'. So perhaps she was damaged by events in her childhood too – although there's no excuse and no prison sentence long enough for anyone who sexually abuses children. Believe me; I know what infinitely terrible harm it does.

# Chapter Seven

One evening, one of the nuns made an announcement: we were all going to learn Irish dancing.

'It will be once a week, every week, on Thursday night,' the nun said. 'And perhaps I should make it clear that this is *not* optional. *Everyone* will attend the classes.'

Most of the girls were excited and immediately started twirling and jigging around the room, although the boys were less pleased. But we all knew we had little choice because, ultimately, we always had to do what we were told.

The first Irish dancing lesson was held in the dining room. All the tables and chairs were pushed back against the walls and a nun stood beside the door to prevent anyone – specifically any of the boys – making a dash for freedom and the preservation of their dignity. Funnily enough though, for someone who had almost perfected a façade of indifference and reluctance to join in with anything, I could feel my stomach churning with what felt like excitement.

Our dance teacher was a young, pretty, dark-haired woman called Sylvia who had a passion for dancing that was infectious. And although I moaned as loudly as any of the other boys to begin with, the truth was that I began to look forward to Thursday evenings.

It turned out that my sister, Teresa, was a natural dancer with a flair for what we were being taught, and she was soon the best of all of us. To my surprise, I got quite good too – although I was never in Teresa's league. Part of the incentive for me was that I grew to like Sylvia and I wanted her to like me, and the best way to achieve that end seemed to be to practise really hard – which I often did with some of the girls – so that by the next lesson I'd learned the steps to the jigs and reels and all the other dances whose names I can't now remember. Then, one day, Sylvia told us that she was entering some of us into a competition – including me.

When the day arrived, I was very nervous, but because I was so determined to do well, I managed to control my nerves and I came second. Sylvia congratulated me warmly and seemed to be genuinely delighted, although I was disappointed. I was so used to being told I was no good at anything – I couldn't even hold my knife and fork in the 'right' hands – that I'd wanted to be able to do just one thing better than anyone else. So, before the next competition, I practised until I could do the dances in my sleep.

Unfortunately, I never really learned when to keep my mouth shut as a child, and long before the day of the competition I'd already told everyone I was going to do better than last time – which meant that I'd be teased and humiliated if I didn't. In the event though, my hard work paid off and I did get the winner's medal. To me, it was like winning gold in the Olympics and I've never forgotten how proud I felt when I ran over to show it to Sylvia, who beamed at me and told me I was 'a winner'.

I took part in lots of competitions after that, and did well in all of them, although anything less than first place always seemed to me like failure. Sylvia did far more for me than teach me the steps of an Irish jig though. She gave me the opportunity to experience what it was like to succeed, and she gave me some of her passion, which is an emotion I don't remember ever having felt previously about anything. On the downside however, I became a bad loser, which is a fault that remains with me to this day.

Apart from the Irish dancing, I didn't get involved with many other activities at Nazareth House, although there were a couple of boys I hung out with sometimes, so I wasn't always entirely on my own. Both of them were boys who were considered by the nuns to be trouble, just like me, and who never seemed to care – although, looking back on it now, perhaps it was just that they were as good as I was at pretending.

One of them, a big lad called Dave Phillips, came up to me while I was getting ready for school one morning and asked, 'D'ya wanna get out of here?' He said it out of the side of his mouth, in a voice like Humphrey Bogart's, and I laughed – until I realised that the question itself was a serious one. I shrugged my shoulders and said, 'Okay.'

When we met a few minutes later, near the laundry, we strolled side by side through the grounds of Nazareth House until we were out of sight of anyone who might be looking out of a window, and then we started to run. And we kept on running – across the fields, where we couldn't be seen from the road – and then, breathless but exhilarated, threw ourselves down on to the rough grass beside a hedge.

When we could breathe again, we talked about what we were going to do, and it wasn't long before we'd reached a unanimous decision: we would smuggle ourselves on to a boat bound for Ireland. But first, we'd go to the corner shop in the village and steal some chocolate.

Shortly afterwards, we were running again, this time with our pockets stuffed full of chocolate bars and pursued by the shopkeeper, the sound of whose wheezing and panting gradually faded into the distance.

As we walked through the fields in the sunshine, it felt as though a weight had been lifted from my shoulders and I was free. Then Dave said, 'I expect the police will be looking for us already,' and although the idea seemed to excite him, it was something I hadn't even thought about and I became immediately frightened and anxious again.

Later, when we were tired of wandering in the countryside, we tried to thumb a lift to London in a lorry. But the only lorry driver who pulled up beside us was so scary that Dave and I looked at each other and then legged it back across the fields, only stopping to roar with laughter when we were a safe distance from the road.

After a while, though, as the sun was dipping below the tops of the trees and the air was turning cold, Dave began to talk about going back to Nazareth House.

'But we've run away,' I told him. 'We can't go back now. They'll go crazy.'

I couldn't believe he was serious. What we'd done wasn't in the same league as being cheeky to a nun, or even punching someone because they called you a bastard. Running away was *really* bad behaviour and I couldn't even begin to think what our punishment would be if we went back.

I wouldn't have agreed to run away at all if I hadn't thought Dave meant it. But carrying on alone wasn't an appealing option for lots of reasons. I was really disappointed with Dave for letting me down. So we argued, and then set off on the long, silent walk back to the trouble I knew would be waiting for us.

We sneaked in through the rear entrance of the building, and got caught before we'd taken more than a few steps along the corridor. Dave was sent upstairs to rejoin his own group, while I was told to go to the cloakroom and wait.

A long, narrow room with a row of steel mesh lockers along one wall, the cloakroom was where we kept our outdoor shoes and coats, and as I paced up and down it, I chewed at the skin around my thumbnail and tried not to think about what was going to happen.

When the door eventually opened, Sister Mary came in with another nun and, standing in front of me with her arms folded, she asked where I'd been.

'Just out,' I said, trying to sound casually confident, but in reality doing little to hide the fear I really felt.

Neither of the nuns said anything as Sister Mary bent down, picked up a shoe and hit me with it on the side of my head, sending me crashing against the metal lockers.

'Do you have no understanding of all the trouble you've caused?' she shouted at me. 'The police have been searching for you all day. Do you think they don't have more important things to do with their time than search for a worthless, evil, selfish child like you, Jerry Coyne?'

The truth was that before Dave had said that the police were probably looking for us, it had never even crossed my mind that they might have become involved, or even that anyone else might be searching for us. I think I just assumed I didn't matter enough for them to bother.

The two nuns were still beating me with shoes when my sister Geraldine walked into the room. I was amazed to see her, and relieved too, because I knew the nuns wouldn't dare to beat me in front of my big sister. I never did find out how Geraldine came to be there. I suppose Mother Superior must have phoned my dad when they couldn't find me, and presumably he'd been at the pub, so Geraldine had come instead.

I was just about to take a step towards her when, without a word and with tears in her eyes, *she* stepped forward and hit me. The force of the blow sent me staggering back against the wall, and I was still reeling from the shock – both physical and emotional – when she turned and marched out of the room.

I suppose I'd hoped that Geraldine would understand why I'd run away, and although I don't know what I'd expected her to do, suddenly I felt more alone than ever, because it seemed that there was no one who was glad to know I was safe. I'd always assumed Geraldine didn't know how the nuns treated me, and that if she had she'd have done something to stop it. But, after that day, I began to wonder if she'd been aware of it all along. Mostly though, I tried not to think about it, because I didn't want to face the possibility that I'd been betrayed by the one person I'd always trusted.

Although I did make the occasional friend amongst the children at Nazareth House and at school, I found it difficult to form relationships with any of the adults I came into contact with – which included my teachers, the nuns and the lay staff at the children's home who cooked and cared for us in various ways. And then, one day, when I got back from school, Judith Harding had joined the staff at Nazareth House.

I liked Judith immediately, and what was really amazing was that she seemed to like me too. She was the only adult I'd encountered who ignored what everyone else said about me and talked to me as though I was a normal human being. She asked me questions about school, about what I liked and didn't like doing, and when I was miserable, she stopped whatever she was doing and concentrated all her efforts on making me smile.

The relationship I developed with Judith was the single most important and significant relationship of my childhood – as well as being the only one that was positive – and I grew to love her more than anything or anyone in the world.

I sometimes cleaned cars for members of staff at the children's home, and I'd spend hours washing, waxing and polishing Judith's little car, until the paintwork was so shiny you could see your face in it. When I'd finished, she'd come outside and admire it, laughing when I challenged her to find one single dirty mark on it and telling me that it was, without doubt, the cleanest car in the whole of the country.

But it was never a good idea for any child at Nazareth House to draw attention to themselves in any way that might arouse jealousy, and when it became apparent to the other children that I was suddenly cheerful and becoming more confident, some of them started to tease me and say – in mocking, sing-song voices – that Judith was my girlfriend. I didn't care though. They could be as spiteful and as stupid as they wanted to be, because I knew they didn't have anyone special in their lives, as I now did, and I could live with their taunts and their envy.

And then a new nun was put in charge of the group of children I was in and, for some reason – perhaps simply because she was unhappy herself, so didn't want to see happiness in other people – she seemed to be determined to destroy the one real friendship I had.

Sister Frances was a small, overweight nun with a face that only God and the most devoted mother could have loved. She had huge hairy moles on her chin, which looked like spiders lying on their backs with their legs stretched out above them, and she wore thick glasses that magnified her eyes and made her look like an angry, startled owl. But it wasn't really her facial features that made her so unattractive; it was the bitter spitefulness of her character and the nasty, small-minded thoughts that were written so clearly on her face.

Although everyone – both children and staff alike – seemed to be targets for Sister Frances's resentment and ill-humour, she particularly hated me, and as soon as she became aware of my friendship with Judith she attempted to warn her off by telling her that any relationship between us was inappropriate.

I know Judith tried to stand up for me and that she was shocked and angered by the implication that there was something 'improper' in our friendship. I was a child, for God's sake, and Judith was a motherly, kind woman who'd realised I was completely starved of affection and had wanted to be nice to me. In the end though, she was forced to bow to the pressure that was being put on her – at least to some extent – and she became more guarded when she spoke to me.

She tried to explain why she had to be careful about

being seen talking to me, and I did try to understand, but I was incredibly hurt and disappointed by the loss of the brief friendship I'd had with the only adult who'd ever shown me any physical affection.

If Judith's maternal kindness wasn't popular with the nuns, maybe they'd have approved more of the way Frank Cameron tried to make friends with some of the boys.

I used to wonder if Frank was employed at Nazareth House in an attempt to keep the boys in order – I wasn't the only one who was unruly and sometimes badly behaved. But although most of the nuns and other members of staff seemed to like him, from the first time I saw him I thought that there was something creepy about him.

Despite the fact that he didn't have any responsibility for the group of children I was in, he chatted to me a few times and was obviously trying to be friendly. Then, one day, he asked me if I'd like to go out with him in his car. Normally, anything that broke the monotony of my life and gave me a chance to get away from the home for a while would have sounded like a great idea, but I didn't like Frank, so I said no, and he shrugged and smiled at me in an odd way.

The next time I saw him, he acted as though nothing had happened and told me that he knew the nuns had it in for me and he understood how I must feel. In fact, he said, he understood *me* and he was on my side. Although Judith had always been good to me and had always cheered me up when I'd got into trouble or was upset for any other reason, she'd never said anything about the nuns at all – negative or otherwise. So it was a new experience for me to hear someone speak out openly like that and I half smiled at him as I said, 'Yeah, well, okay.'

I told myself that he probably couldn't help his peculiar manner and that – as I should know better than anyone – everyone deserves a chance to show their real character. And then, a couple of nights later, I woke up to find him sitting on my bed, staring at me. I almost leapt out of my skin, but when I asked him what the hell he was doing, he said, 'I was worried about you. I just wanted to make sure you were all right. It's okay. Go back to sleep.' Then he stood up and walked out of the room.

There was no denying that it was a very odd thing to have happened, but there were lots of odd things in my life, so I didn't think much more about it – until I woke up again, a few nights later, and he was my stroking my leg through the blankets.

Still half asleep, I struggled to sit up and demanded, 'What the fuck's going on?'

Frank held his finger to his lips and whispered, 'Shhh. It's okay. I heard a noise and I was just checking.'

It was some weeks later when he next came into my room, and on that occasion he woke me up deliberately and asked, 'Are we friends?'

The question and the time he'd chosen to ask it seemed more than a bit strange. But, as I say, I lived in a world where the strange was commonplace, so I told him, 'Yes.'

I could smell alcohol on his breath and although I was still groggy with sleep, I had a flash of sympathy for him. He was probably lonely and just wanted someone to talk to, someone he knew wouldn't snitch on him. I was just starting to feel genuinely sorry for him when he suddenly pushed his hand under the blankets and squeezed my thigh. I shouted and jumped out of bed, and as the boys I shared a room with began to stir and murmur in their sleep, Frank stood up quickly, opened the door and, after checking the corridor, stepped out into it and disappeared.

Not long after that night, I began to hear all sorts of rumours from other children about Frank Cameron's behaviour, but it wasn't until some time later – after I'd already left the home – that he was sacked.

I was still getting into trouble at school, as well as with the nuns, and one day I attacked the deputy head teacher. I was playing a game of tag with some other children when I ran past him and he held out his hand and grabbed me by the hair. I shouted at him, calling him a bastard and telling him to 'fuck off', and, to cut a long story short, it ended up with him chasing me around the dining room, while I tried to slow him down by throwing chairs and anything else that came to hand in his direction.

Whenever those sorts of incidents occurred, it was as though someone had wound me up and I couldn't stop myself until the coil inside me had released every last atom of its energy. On that occasion though, it was still tightly wound when I was caught and dragged off to the head-mistress's office, where I was beaten with a strap until my bottom was raw.

As usual, the headmistress informed the children's home about what had happened, and that night Mother Superior told me angrily that I was completely out of control. After a couple of nuns had beaten me, I lay in my bed with my hands crossed over my chest and prayed that God would forgive me for my sins, even if no mortal being could find it in their heart to do so.

A few days later, I was told I wouldn't be going to school that morning because I had to go to the hospital. When I asked why, one of the nuns said it was because I was going to have a test that would prove I was mad. Some of the other children heard what she said and they began to laugh and point their fingers at me, chanting, 'Jerry Coyne is crazy. Jerry Coyne is crazy.'

After breakfast, while everyone else was setting off to

catch the bus for school, I sat alone in the lounge, trying not to look frightened and racking my brains to think of some way of escaping. But by the time two nuns came in to collect me, the only 'plan' I'd managed to come up with was to tell them I wasn't going to go with them.

'You can't make me,' I shouted at them. 'I'm not mad and I'm not going to have any fucking tests at the fucking hospital.'

Instead of hitting me, as I'd have expected her to do if I hadn't been too close to panic to think at all, one of the nuns just shrugged and said, 'That's fine.' Then she turned her back on me and walked away towards the open door, adding over her shoulder, 'You don't have to come to the hospital if you don't want to. They'll just come here instead, and then you'll be taken to a mental institution, where you'll live for the rest of your life in a padded cell. You'll have to stay there until you're a very old man and they'll give you electric shocks every day. You'll never see daylight or any member of your family again. But if that's what you'd rather do . . .'

She'd already reached the door when I shouted, 'Wait!' and for a moment I didn't think she was going to turn around.

At the hospital, I saw a consultant, who listened while one of the nuns told him about my violence and my bad behaviour and then asked her, politely but very firmly, to wait outside while he spoke to me. Although I could tell the nun was furious, he just pressed the tips of his fingers together and smiled at her. As she hesitated for a moment, two red spots of indignation appeared on her cheeks, and then she stood up, told me to 'be a good boy for the doctor now' and glided out of the room with her head held high.

I curled my fingers around the wooden arms of the chair I was sitting on and glared at the doctor, who smiled at me over the top of his glasses and said, 'There's no reason for you to be frightened.' He opened the thick file of papers on his desk and then looked up at me again as he added, 'You're just here so that we can see if anything can be done to make things a bit better for you.'

But I wasn't fooled; I knew what his game was. He thought he could lull me into a false sense of security so that I'd let him do all the terrible things the nuns had told me about. Well, I wasn't going to be so easily won over. If he wanted to give me electric shocks and do the test that would prove I was crazy, he was going to have a fight on his hands.

So I said nothing. I just tapped my fingers in a quick, persistent rhythm on the arms of the chair and glared at the wall above the top of his head as he picked up another piece of paper from the file and began to read it.

After a moment, he looked up at me again and said, 'You're not a very happy little boy, are you?'

I shrugged my shoulders.

'What do you like doing best?' he asked. 'Playing football? Doing homework?' He laughed and I only just managed not to smile. Then he asked me some questions about my life – about my family, school and whether I liked living at Nazareth House. But although I really wanted to answer some of them, I knew I mustn't drop my guard and say anything at all.

Eventually though, I couldn't stop myself from blurting out, 'I know what you're trying to do. The nuns told me why I'm here. All you want to do is prove I'm mad. Well, I don't care what you do to me. So why don't you just get on with it?'

The doctor looked at me with what seemed to be an expression of genuine sympathy, but I glared back at him.

'No, Jerry,' he said at last. 'No one's trying to prove you're mad. What we're going to do today is . . .'

I wasn't listening. Despite my show of bravado, I was very frightened, and I didn't think I could bear to hear again the gruesome details of what was about to happen to me.

A few minutes later, I was taken to another room, where a nurse smiled as she told me to sit down in a chair. Then she wheeled a machine across the floor towards me and I gripped the arms of the chair so tightly my fingers turned white and began to throb.

The machine had a bunch of wires hanging out of it, and after the nurse had put a cap on my head, she began to plug the ends of the wires into it. And that's when I realised that she was wiring me up for the electric shocks. I began to panic, pulling wildly at the wires and shouting at the nurse, 'I know what you're doing. Don't touch me. Leave me alone. I'm not mad. I don't need electric shocks.'

It took the nurse and the doctor several minutes to calm me down enough for me to be able to listen to what they were saying as they explained that all they were going to do was ask me some questions and watch the shapes that appeared on a sort of TV screen when I answered them. And then it took several more minutes for them to persuade me to believe what they were telling me – or, at least, to allow them to put the cap back on my head and re-attach the wires.

Fortunately, what they said did turn out to be true, although it was still a horrible experience, because I kept expecting to feel the first surge of electricity entering my brain, and all the time I was thinking, *What if what they're doing proves I'm mad and they lock me up somewhere where I'm all alone for the rest of my life and they give me electric shocks every day?*

But I didn't get locked up after all. Instead, at the end

of the test, the doctor smiled at me, handed me a piece of paper covered in wavy lines and said, 'There, take that. You can show it to everyone to prove you're not mad and that there's nothing wrong with your brain.'

Later, I almost shoved the piece of paper into the face of the nun as we stepped out of the main door of the hospital. I told her what the doctor had said, but she just brushed my proof aside with her hand without even glancing at it, and then she narrowed her eyes and looked at me with an expression I couldn't read.

Nothing further was ever said about my visit to the hospital or about the test. But, a few days later, I'd just got back from school in the afternoon when I was told that the doctor who looked after all the children at Nazareth House was waiting to see me.

A new boy had recently come to live at the children's home and we'd hit it off immediately. His name was Sam Oliver and, like me, he didn't care what anyone thought about him – or perhaps I should say that, like me, he *pretended* not to care – and we got up to endless mischief together.

Inevitably, we were always getting into trouble, but it was Sister Mary, in particular, who hated the pair of us with a passion. She'd often refuse to give us any pocket money because of something we'd done and, on those occasions, I'm ashamed to say that we used to steal money from the chapel to spend on sweets and bottles of pop, which we took to our hiding place on the flat roof above the boiler room and laundry. It was great to have a friend to share a laugh with, although we should have known that the nuns would get the upper hand eventually – as they always did.

On that day after school, Sam had to see the doctor too, and he went into the office first, while I waited my turn outside. I'd been standing in the corridor for a few minutes when a nun walked past and I told her, 'I don't need to see the doctor. I'm not sick.' She smiled at me coldly as she said, 'Well, Jerry Coyne, perhaps that's just a matter of opinion. I think we'll let the doctor decide about that, shall we?' And then she walked away.

I didn't get the chance to speak to Sam when he came out, and the doctor didn't answer any of my questions as he pressed the cold metal of his stethoscope against my chest, shone a light into my ears and then told me to stick out my tongue. When the doctor did eventually speak to me, it was to tell me that I needed to take a tablet every day after school. He didn't say what was wrong with me, and when I asked him, he just nodded absently and said, 'The tablet will do the trick.' Then he waved his hand in the direction of the door and I left the room.

The next day, when Sam and I got back from school and were each handed a small, pink tablet and a glass of milk, we looked at each other, shrugged our shoulders, swallowed them and then forgot all about them.

Later that evening, after I'd eaten my tea, I fell asleep on a chair in the lounge. When one of the nuns woke me up to tell me it was bedtime, I felt dizzy and disorientated. I'd never fallen asleep like that before, and when I tried to stand up, I didn't seem to be able to find my balance or make my legs work properly. And it was the same every evening after that. I felt tired almost all the time, and as soon as I'd eaten my tea, I'd fall asleep and have to be woken up so that I could walk up the stairs and fall into bed.

Sam and I had been taking the tablets for several days when it dawned on me that we were the only ones being given them, and that's when I realised we were being deliberately drugged. The next evening, I refused the tablet the nun held out for me, and as she tried to force it into my mouth, I knocked over the glass of milk she'd put down on the table beside her, snatched the tablet out of her hand and threw it into her face.

I didn't trust *anyone*, and when I felt drowsy and couldn't think clearly, I felt even more vulnerable and frightened than normal. So although Sam continued to do as he was told, I was determined not to take the tablets anymore and, to my amazement, after that first night the nuns didn't insist.

It felt as though, for once in my life, I'd won a small victory over them, although what I couldn't understand was why I continued to fall asleep in a chair every evening after I'd eaten my tea. I began to think that maybe there *was* something wrong with me after all and it hadn't been the tablets that had caused my extreme sleepiness and zombie-like state of mind. And then, one evening, I noticed a few specks of pink powder in my mashed potatoes and I realised why the nuns had, so uncharacteristically, appeared to be prepared to let me have my own way.

I was furious – both because they'd tricked me and because I was deeply suspicious of what they were doing to me. I could almost feel the rage like a boiling liquid inside me as I stood up, picked up my plate and hurled it with all my strength against the wall. Sister Mary took a few quick steps towards me, her hands outstretched as if to restrain me, and, without thinking, I reached out, snatched the cowl off her head, threw it on the floor and stamped on it. Then I ran to the food trolley at the end of the table and tipped it over on to its side, sending food and broken china spewing out all over the floor.

I was so angry and frustrated that I'd lost control, and as I shouted and swore, accusing the nuns of trying to kill me, children scattered into all four corners of the room, where they huddled together against the walls, their faces white with shock and fear. But the nuns spoke quietly as they tried to calm me down, assuring me that no one meant me any harm and that all they'd wanted to do was help me – presumably in the same way they'd been 'helping me' on all the many occasions when they'd dragged me from my bed at night and tried to beat the Devil out of me.

I think they must have stopped crushing the tablets into my food, either then or shortly afterwards, and it wasn't long after that incident in the dining room that I was sent to a new primary school.

The school itself was a bit of a dump. Its buildings were mostly wooden huts that looked like something left over from the Second World War – which, in fact, is exactly what they were. Just the look of the place made your heart sink. It felt like the sort of school you'd only be sent to because you'd hit rock bottom and nobody cared anymore where you were or what you were doing.

It was a school for 'problem boys' – i.e. boys like me – and the teachers spent most of their time and energy trying to control us, which meant we got precious little in the way of actual education. We had to do three pieces of work a day – of our own choosing – and if we completed them, we were given stars. Five stars equalled one token, which you could use to 'buy' toys to play with in the afternoon, and which you'd lose if you behaved badly. I was eleven years old, and the prospect of being able to play with toys wasn't much of an incentive to do anything constructive. So there was no real punishment if you were naughty. However, there was one good thing about that school – its headmaster.

He was overweight and bald, except for tufts of hair at the side of his head, and he was always singing or humming cheerfully. In fact, he was a genuinely nice man, the sort of person you couldn't help but like, and he was one of the very few people I encountered during my childhood who treated me as though I was normal. More amazing than that, though, was the fact that he seemed to like me – and, apart from Judith, being liked by someone in authority was something of a new experience for me.

Sometimes, he'd pick me up from Nazareth House on a Saturday morning and take me swimming with his son. Then we'd go back to his house, where his wife would make us something to eat, and in the afternoon I'd play football with his son in the park behind their house.

I'd never had a father figure before, except, perhaps, for my brother John – until I'd realised he probably didn't like me any more than my father did. So I'd never formed a strong attachment to any man, and I suppose the headmaster became a sort of surrogate father to me. I looked forward all week to the Saturdays I spent with him and his family. But, even more importantly, I wanted him to like me and approve of me.

Then, one day, the headmaster asked me, almost casually, how I'd feel about being fostered or adopted. My heart seemed to stop beating and I just stared at him for a moment, unable to believe that he and his family might want me to go and live with them like a real son.

'I've always wanted to live with a family,' I told him, and as I spoke, I made a solemn, silent promise to God that if He allowed this amazing thing to happen, I'd be so good He'd have to keep checking to make sure it was really me.

When I went back to Nazareth House that day after school, I couldn't stop grinning. Still unable to keep my mouth shut, even when commonsense should have told me it would have been a good idea to do so, I told everyone who'd listen – and many who didn't – that I was going to go and live with the headmaster of my school. 'I'll be leaving here really soon,' I said. 'And I won't ever be coming back.'

Every single day after that, I behaved perfectly at school. I didn't once get into trouble and I always put up my hand eagerly whenever the teacher asked for a volunteer to help her to do something. But as the days became weeks and still the headmaster didn't say anything further to me about being fostered or adopted, I became increasingly anxious.

One morning, as I was walking down the corridor at

school, on my way to do an errand for my teacher, the headmaster came whistling and bouncing towards me. I stopped, waiting for him to draw level with me, and then I asked him, nervously, 'About that thing you said the other day, sir . . .'

He looked at me and smiled, then raised his eyebrows and nodded his head encouragingly as he said, 'Yes?'

'About being adopted.' I twisted my fingers together so tightly I could hear my knuckles cracking.

'Ah yes.' The headmaster's smile faded for a moment and when it reappeared it seemed smaller and somehow less convincing. Then he patted my shoulder and said, 'Yes, well, no luck so far. Social services have been trying their best, but they haven't managed to find a suitable family for you yet. Never mind though. Chin up, lad. Who knows what tomorrow will bring, heh?'

As I watched him bounding away from me down the corridor, I felt completely numb. How had I been so stupid as to believe that what the headmaster had meant was that *he* was going to adopt me? His family didn't want me. Why had I ever allowed myself to think they might?

'Who knows what tomorrow will bring?' he'd asked. Well, I knew. It would bring exactly what every single tomorrow of my life had brought: nothing – at least, nothing good. I felt humiliated and embarrassed for having allowed myself to believe otherwise. Most of all, though,

I felt as though I'd taken one step further towards accepting that there was no point in believing in anything, because hope only ever led to hurt and disappointment.

That evening, back at Nazareth House, I was eating my tea when the hurt finally gave way to a rage that built up inside me until it seemed that the room was swathed in mist and I could hear a roar like a hurricane in a tunnel. I stood up, lifted the edge of the table and pushed it with all my might, sending everything on it crashing on to the floor. For a split-second there was silence, and although all eyes were turned towards me, no one moved. Then I shouted, 'Fuck you! Fuck you all!' before allowing myself to be dragged by the arm into a corner of the dining room by Sister Frances.

I stood facing the wall with my hands on my head, while the other children finished their tea, and I was still there when they went to bed. All the muscles in my arms were burning, but I didn't dare put them down, because suddenly I was tired of being in trouble and I didn't want to make things any worse than they already were.

By the time the nuns came for me, I'd lost any last remnants of fighting spirit I might have had and had resigned myself to whatever punishment they had planned for me. For some reason, though, I didn't get a beating on that occasion. Instead, I was taken to the chapel, where I was given a cloth and a bucket of water and told to wash the floor. When I'd finished, Sister Dominic made me do it again, and by the time I was eventually allowed to go to bed, I was so tired I couldn't think about anything, not even the heartbreaking disappointment of discovering that, once again, the nuns had been proved right and no one wanted me.

# Chapter Eight

There was a small cupboard underneath the stairs where the staff kept cleaning equipment and where I was sometimes taken at night. It had very little ventilation, just a few holes in the door, which you could see through if you pressed your eye up close to one of them. I often didn't know what I'd done to deserve to be punished by being shut in there, and the nuns didn't tell me. They just got me out of my bed in the middle of night and opened the door of the cupboard again in time for me to serve on the altar at their early-morning service in the chapel.

In the winter, the cupboard under the stairs was icy cold, but I was never given a blanket, and however much I rocked backwards and forwards trying to get warm, it didn't make any difference. One night, when I'd been banished there for some act of defiance or rudeness, I was so cold I couldn't sleep at all. So, eventually, I slowly eased the door open, checked to make sure that there was no one around and then crept up the stairs to my bedroom, where I dragged a blanket off my bed before running back to the cupboard. The blanket was thin and it didn't really provide me with any warmth, but I wrapped it around me anyway and at last I fell asleep.

In the morning, when a nun opened the door, she must have found me leaning against the wall, fast asleep and still enveloped in the blanket. Furious, she bent down, squeezed her head and shoulders inside the little cupboard and dragged me out by my arm. Still half asleep, I stumbled and cried out as I banged my head against the top of the doorway, and again when the nun slapped me and hissed at me, 'You are an evil child and you will be punished for your deceitfulness.'

When I went to bed that night, I knew they'd be coming for me, so I realised what was happening as soon as I woke up and saw two nuns standing beside my bed. They made me stand in a cold shower until my whole body was blue and aching, and when they turned off the water, they led me – still naked and shivering – down the stairs and pushed me into the little cupboard.

When they'd closed the door, I sat down on the rough, splintered wooden floor, wrapped my arms around my legs and pulled them tight against my chest. It felt as though sharp needles were being stabbed repeatedly into every inch of my skin, and even the bits of my body that were numb still seemed to be able to feel pain.

I don't know how long I'd been in there when the door opened and Sister Josephine reached in and grabbed my arm. My legs were so stiff that it was a few seconds before I was able to stand up and she snapped at me impatiently, 'Get out, child. Hurry up.' I thought she was going to take me back to my bed, but instead she made me kneel in the hall and pray, and then she pushed me into the cupboard again and left me there until morning.

I still have nightmares about being shut in that cupboard. They're so real that when I wake up I'm fighting for breath and I can almost feel the same aching cold in every part of my body. But what are even worse than the nightmares are the flashbacks that are sometimes triggered by cold weather, because when they occur I have to concentrate very hard not to give in to the panic that quickly builds up inside me.

Presumably the nuns at Nazareth House, the headmaster and teachers at my school and my social worker must have decided amongst themselves that my otherwise inexplicably bad behaviour was due to mental issues that required treatment. So they sent me to see a psychologist. Again, I was convinced that they were trying to prove I was mad so they could lock me up in a mental institution, where I'd become someone else's problem and responsibility.

One of the nuns took me to a large house in the centre of Nottingham and I was led into a room, where a man in a grey suit stood up from behind a desk and shook my hand. At one end of the room, near the big bay window that looked out across the garden, there were boxes of toys, which I played with – on that occasion and on several others – while the man in the suit sat at the desk, writing on sheets of paper and occasionally lifting his head to ask me a question.

I didn't tell him much at first – I was too afraid of saying something that might seal my fate and get me sent to a madhouse. But, as the weeks went by, I began to like him, and eventually I told him that the nuns often beat me and that they called me the Devil's child.

It was clear he didn't believe me. I don't know why I'd thought he might. I'd had enough negative experiences by that stage of my life to have crushed all the optimism out of me and I should have realised that no one was ever going to listen to what I said. So he just tut-tutted and told me I should be grateful to all the good people at Nazareth House for taking care of me and for being concerned about my welfare.

'It is wrong of you to tell lies about such good people,' he told me. 'I'm sure they only punish you when you behave badly, and that they do it for your own good.'

I didn't tell him much after that, except for once when

I answered one of his persistent questions and began to tell him about the night the nuns had held me over an open grave. I hadn't ever told anyone about that night, and my whole body was shaking as I described how they'd let me fall into the grave and how I kept having terrifying nightmares about it and sometimes imagined it was happening even when I was wide awake and it was the middle of the day.

I could see immediately from the expression in his eyes that he thought I was making it up. He looked at me impassively for a moment, then shook his head slowly and said, 'You are a boy with a very troubled imagination.'

I was lots of things as a child – troubled certainly, as well as frustrated, unhappy, badly behaved, insecure, frightened, distrustful and very lonely – but I was telling the truth, for all the good it did me.

There must have been about a hundred people at Nazareth House, including the children, the old people, the nuns and the lay staff who worked there, but it often felt as though I might just as well have been entirely on my own. I always seemed to be the odd one out. It didn't help that all the other children went to a different school from the one I went to, which meant I was often excluded from the things they did, or that I had a terrible stammer, responded to feeling hurt or frustrated by becoming angry and was usually left out of their games because I was a bad loser.

We'd sometimes play rounders, which I was good at, although I was always the last to be picked for a team, both because I wasn't very popular and because I was so determined to win that I was unable to hide my disappointment if I didn't. Consequently, rather than taking part, I'd often sit in my hiding place on the roof of the laundry, watching the other children playing and telling myself I didn't care.

Sometimes, I'd think, in an abstract way, about killing myself. But although I didn't want to be alive, I was very scared of dying. The nuns had instilled in all of us the belief that if you're good, you go to heaven when you die, but if you're bad, you spend eternity burning in the fires of hell – and that was *after* you'd been buried deep in the ground in a wooden box!

I'd sometimes sit on my own and try to think of one person who'd miss me or be sorry if I was dead. But there didn't seem to be anyone in the world who'd shed a tear at my graveside – except, perhaps, for Geraldine. It was a very miserable thought, and the only way I could make myself feel any better after I'd thought it was by telling myself that I didn't need anyone anyway, so it didn't matter.

But, of course, it did matter – all of it. It mattered that I was frightened all the time, that I was alone, that everyone seemed to hate me, and that, when I was hurt, I didn't know how to stop myself behaving badly and getting into trouble – and then they hated me even more. Even if anyone *had* ever wanted to include me and talk to me, my stammer was so severe I couldn't really communicate properly anyway. I felt like an outcast, and as the hurt became anger, it built up inside me until it burst out of me and I did something bad. And the funny thing was, no one ever seemed to wonder why.

Then, one day, when everything seemed even more hopeless and pointless than usual, I took a skipping rope from the playroom and walked around the grounds of Nazareth House looking for somewhere to hang myself.

Although I knew exactly what I was doing, it was as though I wasn't in control of my actions. The part of my brain that enabled me to make basic decisions was still working normally, but the part of it that controlled my ability to feel emotion seemed to have shut down. I did hear a voice in my head telling me not to do it at one point, but it was quickly drowned out by the far louder voice urging me on.

I knew I couldn't hang myself from a tree, because all the trees could be seen from the windows of the house. So I continued to wander around the grounds until I noticed a metal overflow pipe on the wall at the back of the laundry that looked as though it was just what I needed to do the job.

I climbed up on to the first part of the laundry roof and reached over to tie the rope around the pipe, tugging on it a few times to make sure it was secure. Then I tied the other end around my neck and stood there, trying to summon up the courage to jump. I must have made at least a dozen nearly-jumps, clenching my fists as the energy slowly built up inside me and then stalled at the last moment. It felt as though my feet were made of lead, or were stuck to the roof with glue so that I couldn't make them move.

And then, suddenly, I was falling. I don't know if I actually jumped or slipped, but, however it happened, I was hanging by my neck and the pain was excruciating. I began to struggle, waving my arms and kicking my legs wildly in the air as I searched for something solid to put my feet on. But there was nothing to support me.

The muscles in my arms were aching, then my legs stopped kicking and my head seemed to be full of something that was forcing all the blood into my ears until I thought they were going to explode. And the next thing I knew, I was lying on the ground, coughing and gasping for air.

It felt as though my neck was on fire, and I was still trying to untie the rope from around it when Sister Dominic walked round the corner of the laundry towards me. She stopped for a moment, looked down at where I was lying in a pathetic little heap on the ground, laughed a nasty sneering laugh and said, 'Maybe you'll have better luck next time.' Then she turned her back on me and walked away.

On another day, when I'd been in trouble, I hid on the roof of the laundry again – it was where I often went when I needed to get away from everyone and think. For some reason, I'd stolen a small knife from the dining room when no one was looking, and I took it out of my pocket, turned it over in my hand a few times and then made a cut on my arm. It wasn't a very big cut and I don't know what made me do it – although I suppose it must have been premeditated, otherwise I wouldn't have stolen the knife.

As I watched the blood slowly seeping from the wound in my skin, it felt as though my emotional pain had been transformed into physical pain, which was somehow being washed out of my body with each bright-red drop of my blood. It was a very strange sensation and, in some ways, a good one, so that cutting myself soon became a regular means of letting out the frustration that often seemed to be trying to choke me.

After the mistake I made when I thought my headmaster and his family wanted to foster or adopt me, my behaviour at school deteriorated and when I was eleven, it was decided that I should go to a 'special' boarding school. Sadly, the word 'special' didn't mean a school like Eton or Harrow, for example, but rather what I think is now called 'a residential school for boys with challenging behaviour'.

It didn't do anything to bolster my self-confidence to know that I was the subject of meetings and negotiations, as all sides – the Catholic Children's Society, Social Services and my father – tried to decide what they could do with me that would enable them to dissociate themselves from any responsibility for my continuing education.

Although my father clearly didn't want to get involved and was happy to leave most of the decisions and arrangements to other people, he did have one stipulation: I must go to a Catholic school. I suppose it was understandable, given the religion he was born into, although perhaps it would have been less so if anyone had taken into account the fantastic job that had been done by the Catholics who'd been taking care of me until then!

My social worker set about contacting Catholic schools far and wide and I think that, initially, the responses from some of them were encouraging. And then, presumably, they read the carefully compiled files of reports about me and, without exception, said that they wouldn't touch me with a barge pole – although I don't suppose they used exactly those words.

Eventually, my social worker spoke to my father again and told him that unless he gave permission for her to start looking at non-Catholic establishments, she was going to recommend that I be sent to live with *him* and that he should be made solely responsible for my future care. I think he'd signed on the bottom line before she'd even finished the sentence.

Coincidentally – I think – it was about that time when my mother came to Nazareth House on one of her irregular and infrequent visits to see me and my sister Teresa. She insisted, as she'd always done, that my father mustn't know she'd been, and she didn't stay for very long. However, while she was there, my social worker decided to consult her about my future – which was bizarre, considering my mother had only bothered to make the long, arduous and very risky journey from London to Nottingham about four times in the last eleven years.

I don't know what pearls of wisdom and maternal insights my mother was able to offer, but I doubt very much that it was because of anything she said that, not long after her brief visit, a school called Knossington Grange, in Leicestershire, agreed to give me an interview.

Knossington Grange was a massive, isolated mansion in its own extensive grounds in the countryside. It hadn't been open as a residential 'education facility' for more than a few months – which perhaps explains why the head-master, Mr Smith, was prepared to consider a boy with my record.

My social worker went with me for the interview at the school, and as we walked into the building, we were met by Mr Smith, a dark-haired, podgy man with an air of unshakeable confidence. He didn't look very scary though, and I remember thinking that it would be a great place to be, not least because I could imagine being able to run rings – both literally and figuratively – around a man like that.

I tuned out while he talked to my social worker, telling her about his plans for the school and what he hoped to be able to achieve for boys 'like young Jerry here', and then I realised he had turned his attention to me.

'So, Jerry,' he said, in a bluffly friendly voice. 'What do you think? Would you like to be one of the first boys to come to Knossington Grange?'

What I wanted to say to him was, 'Does it really matter what I think? Why are you even bothering to ask the question? What difference would it make if I were to say no?' But, instead, I just shrugged my shoulders and stared at the floor. And it was decided that, in view of my overwhelming enthusiasm, I'd start at the school in two months' time.

As the day drew nearer, I had mixed feelings. Although I was profoundly unhappy and lonely at Nazareth House, I suppose I assumed that the treatment I received there was normal for boys like me and that it would probably continue at my new school. So, whereas I had many reasons for being anxious to get away from the children's home, I knew more or less what to expect from the nuns, and the prospect of stepping into the unknown is often more frightening than whatever's familiar to you, however dismal it might be.

My anxiety wasn't helped by the fact that Sister Dominic and Sister Mary, particularly, never missed an opportunity to remind me, with a nasty smile, that 'things will be very different for you at Knossington Grange, Jerry Coyne'. I nearly laughed out loud when Sister Dominic told me there'd be none of the 'kindness' that had been shown to me at Nazareth House. But I didn't feel at all like laughing when she said that the older boys would 'keep me in line' and that I'd soon find out what it was really like to be bullied.

Understandably perhaps, I was a bundle of nerves when the day finally arrived and I set off for my new school. I was accompanied by a nun and my sister Geraldine, but they only stayed for a few minutes when we got there, before leaving me on my own, feeling bereft and deserted – which was odd really, in view of the way I'd been treated by the nuns for as long as I could remember.

Because the school hadn't been running for very long, it was still in the process of building up its numbers and there were only about seven other boys there when I arrived. I was introduced to my housemaster, Mr Johnson, a huge man, about six feet five inches tall, who was very friendly and made jokes as he took me to see the room where I'd be sleeping.

There were four sets of bunks in the bedroom and Mr Johnson pointed to one of the bottom beds and said, 'That's yours, and this is David, who's going to be in the one above you.' He also introduced me to the other boys who'd be sharing the room – a boy called Edward and a chubby lad called Harrison, whose family had dropped him off at the school with enough food to keep us all going for several months. Then he rubbed the palms of his hands together and said, 'Right, well, I'll let you lads get acquainted; then perhaps you'd like to have a look round the grounds and get your bearings.'

Despite his affable good humour, I took an instant dislike to Mr Johnson and I was glad when he left us alone.

I was anxious to give the 'right' impression to the boys in my room – that I was tough and not to be messed with, while at the same time potentially friendly – and although I didn't think about it at the time, I expect they felt exactly the same way. So I was relieved when we seemed to get on with each other quite well, and as soon as we'd unpacked our cases, we went out together to explore the grounds, as Mr Johnson had suggested.

Knossington Grange was an amazing old house surrounded by lawns and woodland, and as we explored, I began to think that it was just possible that everything might be going to be all right after all. Maybe being there would give me the opportunity to reinvent myself, make friends and start my life all over again. The first eleven years hadn't worked out too well, but perhaps I was being offered a new beginning. The thought made me feel both nervous and excited.

Before I'd left Nazareth House, I'd stolen some money from the vestry – just enough to buy a couple of packs of cigarettes, which I offered to the other boys when we were in the woods. I could see I'd scored myself a few points, which I expected to lose again when Mr Johnson suddenly appeared, as if from nowhere, and caught us smoking. I thought he'd give us – or at least me – a beating, so I was amazed when he just raised his eyebrows, took the cigarettes out of our hands, ground them firmly into the soil with the heel of his boot and then walked away without saying a word. He didn't ask for the pack though, and as soon as he'd gone, we all lit another, and then laughed and nodded our agreement when Edward said he thought that things at Knossington Grange might turn out to be 'just fine'.

As time went on and more boys arrived at the school, a pecking order began to develop, and because I was

Jerry Coyne

anxious to make it clear that I wasn't someone anyone would want to bully, I went on a fighting spree. I quickly earned a reputation for fighting anyone, even boys who were almost twice my size, and because I was determined and tenacious by nature and never backed down or gave up, it wasn't long before they all became wary of tackling me.

Unfortunately though, my success at establishing the fact that I wasn't someone you'd want to mess with also had the effect of gaining me a reputation for being violent and unpredictable. And although I liked the feeling of power that gave me, it also resulted in all the other boys deciding it was best to keep away from me. So, once again, I was on my own – until it dawned on me that I needed to lose a few fights in order to fit in better.

The problem with trying to balance things, though, is that sometimes the scales go up and down and you never quite reach the right point. Which is what happened on that occasion, and by the time I wanted to try to assert my position again, I'd lost the edge I'd started with.

When we weren't jostling for position in the hierarchy that was being established amongst the boys, we were attending classes in the prefab building next to the court-yard at the rear of the house. Then, at the end of each school day, Mr Johnson took over the supervision of the junior boys, with help from Mr Bell and, on his evenings off, the housemistress, Sally.

Every night at bedtime, Mr Johnson would tuck us into bed and kiss us as he said goodnight – both of which were completely new experiences for me – and although I continued to be wary of him for a while, it wasn't long before he'd become a father figure to all of us. It soon became clear, though, that he had favourites amongst the boys. He could be nice to you one minute and then, for no reason I could ever work out, he'd turn nasty the next. So although I sometimes thought he liked me, I never really knew where I stood with him.

Gradually, the atmosphere at bedtime changed too. His 'tucking-in' process became almost aggressive and when he kissed me goodnight, he no longer did it in what I imagined to be a 'fatherly' way, but forcefully, without any affection. Then, one night, he slipped his hand under my bedcovers and touched my private parts.

I had just turned twelve and I didn't know what the hell was going on. What he was doing didn't feel right and I didn't like it. But I didn't know what was normal, and because I was afraid of making a fool of myself – or making him angry – by complaining, I didn't say anything and, once again, I began to dread going to bed at night.

However, despite the fear I was developing of Mr Johnson, I gradually settled into the routine at my new school during that first term, and it looked as though things weren't going to be too bad. But when I went back to Nazareth House for the school holiday, it was more obvious than ever that the nuns didn't want me there. Although I tried to keep out of trouble, I know they were urging my social worker to find somewhere else for me to stay. So I was glad when the new term started and I was able to escape back to Knossington Grange, where, even though I sometimes got into trouble, at least no one told me I was evil.

On the first night of the new term, Mr Johnson said goodnight as he tucked me into bed, and then he kissed me on my lips, crushing them against my teeth, and put his hand inside my pyjama trousers.

Without thinking, I plunged my own hand down under the bedcovers and tried to push his away. But he squeezed my private parts painfully, put his other hand over my mouth and nose so that I couldn't breathe and said, in a cold, low voice, 'Keep your mouth shut, or else.' His face was just inches away from mine, and although I couldn't read the expression in his eyes, he sounded angry.

Of all the things the nuns had taught me, the thing they'd taught me best of all was to be afraid. At Nazareth House, I'd been afraid of their beatings; I was still afraid in case the God they seemed to believe in might actually exist; I was afraid of the Devil, of going to sleep at night, and – perhaps most importantly of all – that one day I'd die without anyone ever having loved me. And now I was afraid of Mr Johnson – although perhaps, despite the fact that the nuns had destroyed my self-confidence and convinced me that anything bad that happened was my fault, I couldn't blame them entirely for that.

I knew there was no point struggling, so I nodded my head to indicate I'd heard what Mr Johnson had said to me and that I would keep quiet, and he released some of the pressure of his hand over my mouth. But he continued to touch my private parts for a while, before standing up, wishing us all a cheerful 'goodnight' and turning out the light as he left the room.

After he'd gone, I lay awake for what seemed like hours, trying to work out what had just happened. I didn't know what was 'normal' and I don't think it really crossed my mind to tell anyone what Mr Johnson had done. Not only did I take seriously his threat of 'or else' if I opened my mouth, I also knew instinctively – for some reason I didn't understand – that talking about it would make me vulnerable. And in a school for 'wayward' boys, the one thing you never want to do is let anyone think you're in a weaker position in any way than they are.

At break time the next morning, Mr Johnson opened a window that looked out over the playground and called my name. By the time I'd walked across to the building, he was standing waiting for me in the corridor, and he led the way to an empty bedroom. When he'd shut the door, he turned to look at me and there was a stern expression on his face as he asked, 'Did you tell anyone?'

I knew immediately what he meant and I assured him that I hadn't, adding, 'But I didn't like what you did.'

Before I'd even realised he'd moved, he'd taken a step towards me and had grabbed me by the throat with his right hand. He lifted me up so that my feet were off the ground and then slammed my body against the wall, wrapping the fingers of his other hand around my face and squeezing my cheeks so hard I couldn't breathe.

I began to feel dizzy, and just as I thought I was going to pass out, he pushed his face close to mine and said, very slowly, 'I will do what I want with you and you will say nothing to anyone. If you do, I will kill you.' Then he threw me down on the floor, kicked me once in the stomach and walked out of the room.

For a moment, I lay where he'd dropped me as the familiar feeling of hopelessness and disappointment washed over me again. Was it something about *me*? Did I have something written on my face, some invitation to abuse me that only violent bullies could read? I'd allowed myself to believe that things might work out better for me at Knossington Grange, but it was all starting again and it was going to be no different from being at Nazareth House.

Soon, forcing his hand down inside my pyjamas and touching me in a way that sometimes hurt and sometimes made me feel sick and light-headed had become part of Mr Johnson's nightly ritual. And in the daytime, if he passed me in a corridor or on the stairs, he'd often punch me in the stomach surreptitiously and whisper, 'Tell anyone and I'll kill you. Remember, you're on your own here, you little bastard.'

# Chapter Nine

One night, I woke up to find Mr Johnson sitting on my bed. When I opened my eyes, he picked me up and I remember thinking he smelled like my dad did when he got back from the pub. I was still half asleep as he carried me out of the room, along the corridor and into the boot room, where the floor was cold under my feet when he put me down. Then he ripped my pyjamas off me, and suddenly I was fully awake. I tried to fight him off, but he was a big man and I was just a small, skinny twelve-year-old child, and he barely even seemed to notice.

He started touching me, doing things to me I still can't bear to talk about, and when he'd finished, he picked me up by the throat and slammed me against the wall. His hand was compressing my windpipe so that I couldn't breathe, and I began to kick out at him wildly. But it was as though I weighed nothing at all, and he continued to hold me up against the wall with one hand as he told me,

'This is our little secret. Keep it, or I will make your life a misery.' Then he laughed and released his grip around my throat, dropping me to the floor and bending down over me as he added scornfully, 'No one would believe you anyway.'

I knew he was right. I'd rarely spoken to anyone about the brutality of the nuns' treatment of me over the last eight years, and the few people I had tried to tell either hadn't listened or hadn't believed me. So there didn't seem to be any point in telling anyone about what Mr Johnson was doing. I just did what I always did when I was very unhappy and couldn't deal with the emotions that were building up inside me: I started behaving badly and getting into trouble.

I retreated into my own little world, just like I'd done at Nazareth House, and pretended – to myself as well as to everyone else – that I didn't care about anyone or anything. And as the conflict inside me grew more turbulent, my stammer became steadily worse – almost as though my subconscious was providing me with an excuse for isolating myself from other people.

The headmaster had an open-door policy and often reminded us that we could talk to him about anything at any time; all we had to do was go to his office and knock on the door. I *did* think about doing that, or telling one of the other members of staff at the school, most of whom were good people. But I'd learned from experience that adults tend to stick together, particularly when a child criticises one of them, so it didn't seem to be a real option. I didn't know who I could trust – or, to put it more accurately, I didn't trust anyone. So, in the end, I didn't manage to summon the courage to tell the headmaster or anyone else about what was happening.

Despite Mr Johnson's often unpredictable behaviour, he was good at manipulating the junior boys. Some of them would almost fight each other for the privilege of sitting on his knee in the evenings when we watched television, and although I never joined in the clamour for his attention, he sometimes looked at me as he patted his leg and said, 'Come on, lad, sit here with me.' I tried to avoid it, but he'd just say it again, more firmly, and as well as being afraid of him, I didn't want the other boys to wonder why I was refusing.

He always insisted on the overhead light being turned off while we watched TV, but you could see quite clearly in the light from the screen that his hands were inside the pyjamas of whichever boy was sitting on his knee. His favourite – the one who won the scramble to sit on his lap more often than any of the others – was a small boy with a fiery temper whom I was always having run-ins with, as a result of which I took many slaps and punches from Mr Johnson.

One Friday evening, we were in bed when Mr Johnson came into the room and started handing out chocolate bars. As he dropped one into my eagerly outstretched hand, he leaned over and whispered in my ear, 'I'm coming for you tonight, you little bastard.'

I stayed awake for as long as I could after the light was turned out, but I must have been asleep when he put his hand over my nose and mouth, and I woke up just as he was lifting me out of my bed. He carried me up the stairs to the art room, which was on the top floor of the building, and when he put me down, I just stood there, rigid with fear, as he thrust a cloth into my mouth and tied my hands behind my back. He hadn't turned on a light, and the glow of the moon made eerie outlines and shadows on the walls.

Suddenly, Johnson put his face so close to mine I could feel the heat of his breath on my cheek. As the stench of alcohol and stale cigarettes filled my nostrils, he put one hand around my throat, lifted me up until my head seemed to be almost touching the ceiling and, with his other hand, removed my pyjamas. He squeezed my private parts until tears were streaming down my cheeks and I almost passed out with the pain. Then he threw me, head first, on to a table.

The art room was on the same floor as the staff living quarters, and the sound of my body thudding on to the table must have woken someone up, because a few seconds later, the darkness under the door became a sliver of light. Johnson held a finger to his lips and I froze, barely daring to breathe, until the light in the corridor outside went off and we heard the sound of a door closing further down the landing.

The art room was divided in two, and when Johnson was certain that the immediate danger of being discovered had passed, he picked me up and carried me into the inner room, gently closing the door behind us with his foot.

I was still bound and gagged, so my scream was only in my head when he threw me up against a wall and then kicked me as I slid down it on to the floor. Dragging me to my feet by my hair, he bent down so that his face was on a level with mine and said, 'Do you see, you little bastard? I can do whatever I want with you, anytime I want to do it.' He punched me in the stomach, then banged my head repeatedly against a wooden pillar in the middle of the room, and when I was so dizzy I thought I was going to pass out, he dropped me on to the floor as if I were a discarded rag, took all his clothes off and sat down beside me to roll a cigarette.

As he smoked it, he told me, 'I'm the only person in the world who loves you. But never forget that I can kill you any time I choose.'

Although I couldn't make any sense of his claim to love

me, I had absolutely no reason to doubt that he could – and would – kill me if I didn't do what he told me to do. I lay on the floor whimpering and feeling even more frightened and alone than I'd done on the nights when the nuns had dragged me from my bed and beaten me.

When Johnson had finished his cigarette, he untied my hands and pulled me across the floor to a wooden post in the middle of the room. I was shivering and snivelling as he tied a cord around my neck and then lifted me up so that he could attach the other end of it to a hook which was embedded at a height of about six feet up the post. I was too shocked by what he'd already done to me even to struggle. But when he let go of me and I felt the cord tighten around my neck, I began to panic and to thrash about wildly, which only made things worse.

It was probably just a few seconds before everything in the room turned black and I stopped struggling as all the muscles in my body went limp. But at the very moment when I realised I was going to die, Johnson must have lifted me up just far enough to take the weight off the cord so that I could gasp for air.

'Look at me,' Johnson said. He had to repeat the words several times before his voice finally penetrated the panic that was swirling around in my head like fog, and when I looked up into his face, he asked, 'Should I let you die?' I shook my head vigorously from side to side and he laughed as he said, 'Hmm, I can't make my mind up.'

Abruptly, he let me go, and this time I didn't have enough strength left in my body to kick my legs. The last thing I remember is hearing a strangled, wheezing sound as the air escaped from my lungs, and then I was lying on the floor with Johnson bending over me saying, 'Tell me that you love me. Say it! Tell me you want me to make love to you.'

For a moment, I couldn't work out where I was. Then I remembered what had happened and I looked up silently into Johnson's face. But he was relentless in his determination and, digging his fingers into the hot, tender skin around my throat, he kept repeating over and over again, 'Go on, say it,' until finally I did.

I lay on the mattress against the wall and cried while he did horrible, disgusting things to me that hurt me and made me feel sick with shame, for reasons I didn't understand. When he'd finished, it was almost as though the shock and pain that filled my mind had blotted out my ability to think, and for a while I stayed completely still and Johnson lay beside me, stroking my hair.

When I stood up, I loosened the cord around my neck so that I could lift it over my head, walked across the room and opened the door that led into the outer art room. As I bent down to pick up my pyjamas from the floor, I felt something trickling down my legs and when I touched it, I realised it was blood.

I cried out before I could stop myself and Johnson appeared immediately in the doorway between the two rooms. I tried to tell him about the blood, but I was stuttering so badly I couldn't push the words out of my mouth. He didn't need to hear them though, because he could see clearly the state I was in, and he began to panic. Picking me up, he carried me down the stairs to a bathroom, whispering to me that everything would be all right – although perhaps he was trying to reassure himself as much as me. After he'd cleaned me up, he took me back to my bed, and as he tucked the covers around my shaking body, he warned me once again not to tell anyone about 'our secret'. Then he tiptoed out of the bedroom and left me alone in the dark.

The next morning, I wanted to believe it had all been a horrible dream, but what had happened to me that night was way beyond the realms of my imagination, waking or sleeping. For the rest of that day, it felt as though my mind was full of something dense and impenetrable and I couldn't concentrate in any of my lessons. I knew I mustn't do or say anything that would give any of the other boys a clue that something was wrong, and I was playing football at morning break when Mr Johnson appeared and called out my name.

I walked across the playground towards him, and as soon as I was within arm's reach, he pulled me out of sight around the corner of the school building and asked if I'd spoken to anyone. I swore to him that I hadn't and then I told him, 'But it hurts really badly and I *will* tell someone if you ever do that again.'

It was a mistake I regretted immediately. Mr Johnson's face turned bright red and he grabbed me by the throat as he hissed, 'Next time, I'll leave you hanging there until you're dead.' Then he slapped me across the head with such force that he knocked me to the ground, and when I looked up again, I saw the headmaster walking towards us.

For a moment, Mr Smith stood staring down at me with a quizzical expression, and then he turned to Mr Johnson and asked, 'Is there a problem? What's going on?'

'The little bastard kicked me, Headmaster,' Mr Johnson answered, without missing a beat.

'I d . . . d . . . didn't,' I stuttered, standing up and edging instinctively away from him.

'Don't be ridiculous, boy,' Mr Smith snapped at me. 'Now get along to your next lesson. Hurry up now.'

I turned to walk away and when I glanced back at Mr Johnson, he raised one eyebrow and smirked at me.

Many of the confrontations I had at school – both with other boys and with some of the teachers – were caused, either directly or indirectly, by my stammer. I stammered and stuttered all the time – although it was worse when I was particularly upset or frustrated – and I was often reluctant to speak at all. But an even more significant factor in my inability to concentrate and my almost total lack of progress in class was what Mr Johnson was doing to me on what had become a regular basis.

My class teacher was a man with a good sense of humour, and I looked up to him and wanted to do well for him. But it was too late for me to catch up the ground I'd already lost so that I could reach the stage I should have been at in my education. Although it's possible that I could have done better if I'd had some more individual attention, the school was full of damaged, demanding boys with special needs of one sort or another, and none of the teachers had time to spare for coaxing and cajoling just one of us into learning something useful.

Apart from anything else, all our teachers spent a good percentage of the lessons restraining boys and breaking up fights, which meant they didn't have much time left over for straightforward teaching. So I suppose we were our own worst enemies in terms of equipping ourselves for later life and trying to break the pattern that was already set for us so that we stood a chance of getting decent jobs.

One of the only times I felt as though I hadn't already failed at everything was when I was playing football. I loved football, and because all the lads at Knossington Grange had problems, my hatred of losing didn't exclude me from team games, as it had done at Nazareth House. The surface in the playground where we played football every break time and after school was concrete, but that didn't stop me diving across the goal to make a save, and I soon gained a reputation as 'the mad goalkeeper'.

When I played football, it was as though the rest of the world didn't exist. There was no Mr Johnson, creeping like an evil predator into my bedroom at night and carrying me up to the art room or his own bedroom. There were no nuns to remind me constantly that I was the spawn of the Devil and no one wanted me, and no parents who'd abandoned me and who were living proof of the fact that what the nuns said was true. For the precious minutes when I stood in front of the goal and felt the thrill of excitement as the ball came closer, I was no longer conscious of any of those things and I felt almost happy.

By the end of the term, the nuns had finally got their way and I was sent to spend the school holiday at a council-run children's home in Nottingham called Wollaton House, and never returned to Nazareth House again.

Although some of the white lads at Wollaton House were about my size, most of the black boys were huge, and I soon learned that the very distinct pecking order that existed there didn't really involve the white boys at all. On the day I arrived, I'd only been in the building for a few minutes when a black lad walked up to me and, without any warning, got me in a headlock. Luckily, I managed to struggle free and he laughed as he gave me a cigarette and told me, 'You can look after yourself pretty well for such a puny kid.' And although I didn't fully understand the significance of what had just happened, it soon became clear that he'd stamped his seal of approval on me, thereby protecting me against any of the other boys who might have planned to test me out.

Wollaton House was one of the noisiest places I'd ever been to, and it was very intimidating. I couldn't help laughing to myself at the thought that if the nuns believed *I* was trouble, they should spend a day with some of the lads there, most of whom walked round openly smoking cigarettes and never spoke without swearing.

As well as my ability to wriggle out of a headlock, my skills as a goalkeeper came in handy too, and I'd often play for two or three hours at a time with a boy who was a really keen, talented footballer and who appreciated the chance to practise his shots. So, much to my surprise, I liked being at Wollaton House. In fact, it was the only place I could ever remember being where I came anywhere close to relaxing and feeling as though I could be myself.

Most importantly of all though, Wollaton provided me

with somewhere to escape from the huge and increasing stresses of being at Knossington Grange. I'd always dreaded going back to Nazareth House at the end of term, but now, for the first time in my life, I began to look forward to the school holidays.

The start of the next term was a different matter however. I dreaded it, and by the time the bus drove through the school gates my stomach was churning, my body was drenched in sweat and I felt sick. For the last few days, I'd been praying to the God I no longer believed in that something would happen to change things. My favoured option was that when the bus stopped outside the main entrance of the school building, the headmaster would be waiting to tell us that we had a new housemaster. In my head, I could hear him say, in the tone of voice he always used when telling us something serious or important, 'Unfortunately, boys, Mr Johnson has had to leave the school and will never be coming back.'

But it was Mr Johnson who was standing in the car park – as I'd really known he would be. He looked like the lord of the manor, his hands clasped in front of him and a big smile on his face as he welcomed us all back to school. I jumped off the bus, trying to dodge out of his way, but he caught me by the arm and told me how much he'd missed me. And that's when I knew with certainty that nothing was going to change: the new term was going to be just like the last one, and I didn't know how I was going to get through it.

One morning, Mr Johnson slipped ten cigarettes and a box of matches into my pocket and said, 'You can pay for them later.' I dodged around the school for the rest of the day, trying to keep out of his way and even missing lunch to avoid him. But by teatime I was hungry and I reasoned to myself that I'd be safe in a dining room full of people. As I ate my tea, I watched him laughing and joking with boys and other members of staff, and it felt as though dozens of wasps were hovering just above my skin.

That night, when we went to bed, I tried to stay awake, but I was tired and my eyelids kept drooping. Every few minutes, my eyes would snap open again and I'd realise I'd been asleep, until eventually I got up and, with some ill-thought-out idea that it would protect me against Mr Johnson when he came, put on some clothes over my pyjamas.

I don't remember being lifted out of my bed and when I woke up, I was already in the inner art room. Almost dropping me on the floor, Johnson demanded angrily, 'Why have you gone to bed in your clothes?' But he didn't wait for an answer before ripping them off and tying my hands behind my back.

'Please, please don't hurt me,' I begged him, and when

he grabbed me by the throat and said, 'If you don't shut up, I'll kill you,' I knew he meant it, so I tried to stop shivering and crying.

I couldn't swallow, because he still had his hand around my neck, and I was just on the verge of giving in to the suffocating panic that was building up inside me when he released his grip, walked across the room, lifted up one of the sheets that were tossed in a pile in a corner and picked up a bottle.

'Drink it,' he said, holding the bottle up to my lips.

The strong smell of whisky made me retch and I turned my head away and said, 'No, p . . . p . . . please, I . . .'

'Drink it!' he shouted, twisting his fingers in my hair and pulling my head back as he forced the top of the bottle into my mouth so violently he almost cracked my teeth.

The taste was horrible and when I began to choke and cough, he clamped his hand over my mouth and told me to be quiet. Then he made me drink more and more of the whisky until it felt as though my chest was on fire and the room began to spin. I hadn't been in any position to defend myself against him before, but this time I felt so weak it seemed as though I had no control over any part of my body.

Johnson dragged me across the room by my hair and started banging my head against the wooden post. I must have passed out, because the next thing I was aware of was lying on my stomach on the floor being violently sick. I thought I was going to die, but, eventually, when I'd spewed out the entire contents of my stomach – as well as what felt like every ounce of liquid in my body – I managed to turn on to my side.

As well as feeling sick and having a foul taste in my mouth, I was dizzy and there seemed to be pain in every part of me. And that's when I realised that Johnson had raped me while I was unconscious.

He was sitting a couple of feet away from me, smoking a roll-up, and when I looked at him, he must have been able to see the hatred in my eyes, because he suddenly reached out his hand, hit me across the side of my head and said, 'Don't you look at me like that, you little bastard. You don't have anyone else in the world except me. No one else loves you, not even your own family.' Then he laughed, as if he'd said something funny, lit another roll-up and handed it to me.

He'd untied my hands while I was unconscious, and I sat up and smoked the cigarette he'd given me. My brain wasn't working properly and I still felt queasy and disorientated, but even through the haze of confusion, I knew I had no basis on which to argue with him. After all, he was right about my family: they cared so little about me that I hadn't seen any of them for months.

And there was certainly no one else who was going to fight my corner or try to protect me. So what was the point in anything? I seemed to have been fighting all my life without ever having won any of the battles that really mattered.

The first time I tried to stand up, the room began to swirl around me so fast that I lost my balance and sat down again with a thud. I managed to get to my feet on the second attempt, and as I put on my clothes, Johnson kept talking. I didn't really listen to what he was saying – it was more drivel about how he was the only person who loved me – but when I was dressed, I walked across the room and, pausing with my hand on the door handle, I turned to look at him, took a deep breath and said quietly, 'Don't do this again.'

Although I'd intended to open the door and walk out of the room before he had time to react, I hadn't even turned the handle before he'd leapt to his feet, bounded across the floor and grabbed me by the throat.

'Are you stupid?' he hissed at me, his eyes bulging with fury. 'Will you never learn?'

The blood was pounding in my ears as Johnson tied a cord around my neck, carried me back across the room to the wooden post, slipped the other end of the cord over the hook and began to abuse me again. This time though, I felt completely calm. Perhaps I'd reached the point of not caring anymore, or perhaps I was just too drunk to be able to think at all.

My arms hung loosely at my sides and I didn't struggle. Even when the cord began to tighten around my neck, my overriding feeling was relief at the thought that it was all about to be over. But then, just before I lapsed into unconsciousness, he unhooked me and carried me back to my bed.

In the morning, when I woke up from a deep, dreamless sleep, there were a thousand sledgehammers banging in my head, and I almost cried with the disappointment of knowing I was still alive.

Stories about Mr Johnson's sexual preferences were already rife amongst the boys in the school, and when they filtered through to the teachers and we were told to stop spreading vicious rumours, he must have felt that he was safe. Certainly, from my own point of view, my silence about what he was doing to me was more or less guaranteed by the fact that I knew the probable outcome if I said anything: the headmaster and teachers wouldn't believe me and the other boys would ridicule and bully me, at best. And as I already had enough problems for any child to have to deal with, I wasn't going to add to them deliberately.

I suppose most people accept the things they can't change about their lives. If you're starving during a famine

Jerry Coyne

in Africa, I don't imagine you spend much time wishing you were somewhere else. You live where you live, that's your life, and that's what's happening to you. There's nothing you can do to alter the facts, so you just have to get on with it and wait to see what fate has in store for you.

And maybe that's even more the case for children: wherever they are and whatever the circumstances of their childhood, they do what they're told to do and they accept whatever's happening in their lives as 'normal'. They've never had any experience of being able to change things, so they don't have any reason to believe they can. That's how I felt: this was the life I was living and I had to do what I was told by the people who had power over me – which included almost everyone. It was just unfortunate that one of those people was an evil, abusive paedophile, who happened to be the man whose responsibility it was to take care of me – and dozens of other little boys – and tuck me into bed at night. That was just the way it was. I was used to being afraid – in fact, I couldn't remember any time in my life when I hadn't been frightened – so I might as well learn to accept it.

While I was at Knossington Grange, I discovered that – apart from throwing myself across the mouth of a goal with a combination of skill and reckless abandon – there was one other thing I was good at. Running proved to be my one natural talent, and the highlight of every week for me was the cross-country run. I loved the sensation of running and the feeling of freedom it gave me, and I loved the novelty of being good at something.

Once I started to run, I felt as though I could keep going all day, and there wasn't a boy in the school – neither junior nor senior – who could beat me at cross-country. I entered every running race at our annual sports day – 800 metres, 1500 metres, 5000 metres – and I won them all, except the sprint races, which I wasn't so good at. For a while, I even dreamed of taking part in the Olympics, but I'd already been labelled as a 'non-achiever' and so I don't think it even crossed anyone's mind to support or encourage me.

I did have one reason to be grateful to the headmaster though. My stammer had become so bad that I was virtually unable to communicate at all, and one day he told me that he'd arranged for me to go on a week's intensive speech therapy course. I think he did genuinely want to help me, and although I was apprehensive and initially reluctant to go on the course, there was such a marked improvement in my speech by the end of the week that I was really excited.

Mr Smith came to pick me up on the last day and he was clearly as amazed as I was at the progress I'd made. And so was everyone else at Knossington Grange. Whereas

I usually avoided talking unless I had to – not least because I hated the sound of my own stuttering, stupid voice – I suddenly became a boy who had something to say about everything, and I think I had more conversations in the next few days than I'd had in my entire life!

Unfortunately, though, the improvement didn't last very long. I needed regular therapy sessions to maintain the progress I'd made, and without them I quickly began to forget the techniques I'd been taught, until it seemed that the harder I tried not to, the more I stammered. I'd had a glimpse of what it was like to be able to speak normally and not be overwhelmed by frustration and embarrassment whenever I tried to say something, so I asked Mr Smith if I could have more therapy, and he promised he'd look into it. But I never heard anything more about it, and very soon I was almost back to square one – the only difference being that now that I knew it was possible for me to speak without stammering, I was even more frustrated than ever.

# Chapter Ten

The school had an outdoor swimming pool, which was cleaned and filled with water at the start of every summer. Although it was primarily for use by the senior boys in the evenings, the juniors swam in it sometimes too, supervised by Mr Johnson, who would stand watching us with a smirk on his face as we changed into our swimming trunks.

One summer evening, I got into a fight with another boy while we were playing in the swimming pool and as we both got out of the water, he punched me, so I kicked him. Immediately, Mr Johnson came running up to us and slapped me so hard I fell backwards into a hedge. My skin was burning as if I'd been stung and I had scratches all over my body, so when Mr Johnson asked if it hurt, I told him it did.

'You need to cool off,' he said, and although he didn't sound angry, he suddenly grabbed me by the hair, swung me round a couple of times and then threw me into the swimming pool. He took me completely by surprise, so I didn't have a chance to hold my breath before I hit the water, and as I clawed my way to the surface, it felt as though my lungs were going to burst.

Still choking and spluttering, I swam to the side of the pool, and I was holding on to the rail, coughing up water, when Mr Johnson sent all the other boys scurrying back towards the main building of the school, their clothes clutched damply under their arms. He reached down to pull me out on to the concrete paving stones and then he dragged me towards a little hill that separated the pool from a wooded area, which was out of bounds because some of its trees were rotten and in danger of falling down.

At the top of the hill, he gave me a back-hander that sent me tumbling down, head over heels, towards the trees. When I came to a halt, I was covered in dirt and my head was spinning, but before I could even work out which way was up, Johnson was running down the slope towards me.

As he stood looking down at me, laughing, I glanced around and realised we were completely hidden from the school buildings. Johnson must have known what I was doing, because he bent down, put his hand inside my swimming trunks, squeezed my private parts and said, 'No one can see us here. So if I dug a hole and buried you in it, no one would ever know.' Then he half carried me back up the hill, threw me into the swimming pool and, almost spitting the words at me, told me, 'You're filthy. Clean yourself up.'

Mr Johnson had set up a Cub Scout group for the juniors. Meetings were held every Thursday evening and attendance was compulsory. I hated them. I knew enough to know that you were supposed to do things to earn badges, but Mr Johnson handed them out to the boys he liked for doing absolutely nothing. It was embarrassing, particularly for one boy, who was Mr Johnson's favourite and whose uniform ended up looking like a patchwork quilt.

When Mr Johnson decided to set up a camp in a field above the school, we all thought it was stupid – a bit like being told you were going on a week's holiday only to find that the tent had been pitched in your own garden. In fact, though, camping was good fun – as long as you managed to avoid being caught on your own with him. We did loads of activities, and while other members of staff were around, Mr Johnson organised games of volley-ball, football and rounders – although as soon they'd gone and he was alone with us, it was a different matter.

One evening, he split us up into two groups and told us, 'Whichever group collects the most firewood will win a prize,' and before he'd even finished speaking, we were shooting off into the trees, whooping excitedly. Searching for firewood was fun for a while, but it wasn't long before a small group of us decided to find somewhere to have a sneaky cigarette. We walked away from the area where the other boys were still picking up bits of wood and had just seen what looked like a suitably secluded spot, when we almost literally tripped over Johnson and a boy called Tom.

They were crouched behind a bush and it was obvious what Johnson was doing. For a moment, he just stared at us, too startled to react, but he quickly gathered his wits and shouted at Tom and the rest of us to get a move on and pick up some more wood or there'd be no supper for anyone.

Later, when we were building the fire, several of the boys were muttering to each other about how Johnson had been found 'bumming' some boy in the woods. And although that was a gross exaggeration of what we'd actually seen, I did wonder what might have happened to Tom if we hadn't stumbled across them when we did.

A couple of nights later, I got up when everyone was asleep, crawled out of the tent and was tiptoeing towards the toilet behind the pavilion when I saw a little lad having a pee while Johnson knelt on the ground beside him and seemed to be cuddling him. They didn't see me, so I turned round and crept back to my tent, having decided that, all things considered, my need to go to the loo wasn't as urgent as I'd thought it was and could certainly wait until morning.

But the next night it was my turn. I woke up to find Johnson standing in the tent beside me and as I opened my eyes, he put his finger to his lips. Then he picked me up and carried me to his car, where he half lifted, half pushed me on to the back seat before getting in beside me and closing the door.

I was frightened, but being more or less out in the open – rather than shut away behind two doors in the art room, as we usually were – gave me the courage to try to resist him. I told him to leave me alone and that I wanted to go back to bed. But he just laughed, opened a can of beer and handed it to me as though I hadn't even spoken. 'Drink it,' he said and when I hesitated, he almost slammed the can into my face as he repeated, 'Drink it. All of it.'

The beer tasted bitter and disgusting, but I took a gulp and then another, while Johnson rolled two cigarettes, lit them both and handed one to me.

'You know,' he said, in a casual, conversational tone, 'if only you could learn to do what you're told, I could make your life here a great deal better than it is.' He reached across and pushed my hand towards my mouth so that I drained the last of the beer from the can and then he opened another and passed it to me.

By the time I'd drunk the second can, I was feeling

dizzy and sick. So I was only vaguely aware of what was happening when Johnson reached forward between the front seats of the car and then pushed a piece of cloth into my mouth. I gagged and, thinking that the material was going to get stuck in my throat and choke me, I tried to take hold of the end of it. But, for some reason, I didn't seem to be able to control the movement of my limbs, and my fingers kept closing on nothing as I waved them ineffectually in front of my mouth.

Clearly, I was drunk, although I was still sober enough to feel the pain when Johnson raped me – at least until I passed out. The next thing I knew, I was back in the tent and one of the other boys was pushing me with his foot and telling me that if I didn't get up right away, I'd miss breakfast.

I managed to avoid Mr Johnson all morning, until I made the mistake of sneaking off into the woods to have a cigarette. I was certain no one had seen me, but when I heard the sound of a twig snapping, I spun round and he was already standing just a few feet away from me.

I dropped the cigarette on the ground and tried to make a run for it. But he was surprisingly agile and quick on his feet for such a large man, and I'd barely taken a few steps before he grabbed me by the throat and slammed me up against a tree.

'Never forget how easy it would be for me to kill you.'

He spat the words into my face. 'Now, repeat after me, "I promise I won't tell anyone our secret".'

So I said it, although he didn't really need to make me promise, because I was far too afraid of him and far too disgusted by the things he did to me to have told anyone about them.

When he released his grip around my neck, I dropped to the ground, and as I watched him walk away, he stopped for a moment, looked over his shoulder and said, 'I've got a shovel in the back of the car. I could dig a grave for you in less than five minutes.' And I believed him, just as I believed that even if I did tell the headmaster or someone else about the secret I so reluctantly shared with him, they wouldn't be able to protect me from what he'd do to me when he found out.

I'd realised by that time that it wasn't just me Johnson was sexually abusing – although I still didn't really understand what he was doing. He controlled all the boys in his care by being in turn aggressive, so that we were afraid of him, and loving, like the father I – and probably most of the others – had never had. We were all children who'd been damaged in some way and we all came from backgrounds that were deprived – emotionally, intellectually, financially or in other ways – and Mr Johnson used our common need for love and affection to manipulate us.

In the summer, Knossington Grange held an open day,

which was attended by parents from all over the country and – to my complete amazement – by my brother John and a couple of his friends. I couldn't believe it when I saw John walking up the driveway. I was so excited I only just managed to stop myself running towards him and throwing my arms around his neck. It was as though his presence at the school gave me an identity I'd never previously had. I felt so proud to have him there and to be able to show the other boys that I wasn't all alone and unloved; I had someone too – someone who was far more impressive than many of the other visitors who were there that day.

The grounds of the school were full of stalls and activities such as archery and shooting, and the place was buzzing with the sound of people enjoying themselves. When Mr Johnson came over and introduced himself to John, I was anxious – as I always was whenever he became involved in anything. But the fact that he'd now met my brother and could see that I wasn't unloved and all alone in the world, as he was always telling me I was, gave me a huge sense of satisfaction. I should have known that it would be short-lived though, and I stared at my shoes, trying not to cry, as I listened to him running me down to John and laughing as he described to my brother the techniques he used to keep me under control.

A few minutes later, when John's attention was briefly

being taken up by something else, Mr Johnson murmured at me out of the side of his mouth, 'Go for a fucking cigarette. Now! I want to talk to your brother.' I knew there was no point arguing, so I walked away from them across the grass, stood nervously behind a classroom, out of sight of all the guests, and lit a cigarette.

A couple of minutes later, Mr Johnson appeared around the corner of the building, grabbed me by the neck and pushed me up against the wall as he said, 'I do hope you're not thinking about doing anything silly.'

I looked away from him and muttered, 'I've said nothing.'

'Good', he snapped. 'Keep it that way. Don't forget, your brother will be going home soon, and when he's gone, you'll still be here. And you know that if you *do* say anything, I'll kill you.' Then he turned and walked away, smoothing the front of his shirt with his hands.

I spent the rest of the afternoon with John, trying to make the most of having him there. But I was so anxious for him to enjoy himself that I couldn't relax, and as I watched him drive away with his friends at the end of the day, I was worried in case he hadn't had a good time and might wish he hadn't come. Or, even worse, that he might never want to come again.

Mr Johnson had an uncanny ability to guess what was worrying you and make use of it, and that evening he started teasing me in front of the other boys, saying, 'Your brother won't want to be associated with you now that I've told him the truth about you. What's the betting he never comes to see you again?'

We all took our cue from Mr Johnson. For example, if he said someone was 'a good boy', they became popular; whereas any boy he decided to make look bad was shunned and hated by everyone else. He was the one person whose approval you needed if you were going to stand any chance of leading a reasonable life at school. So when he made his mean, spiteful comments to me about my brother, it gave some of the other boys the perfect opportunity to get back at me for boasting. Encouraged by Mr Johnson, they began to laugh at me, until, with my cheeks flushed with humiliation and embarrassment, I turned and shouted at him to 'fuck off', and he sent me to bed.

Later, when I knew the other boys would be watching television, my bedroom door opened and Mr Johnson came into the room. I was still hurt and angry because of what he'd said and because he'd taken away all the pleasure I'd had from my brother's visit, and I refused to look at him. But instead of shouting at me, he sat down on the bed beside me and told me he was sorry for saying all those things about John.

I was amazed to hear him apologise, although I should have known better than to think he'd come to my room merely to say he was sorry. As I looked up at him, he said, 'But I think you should know the truth. I had to beg your brother to come to the open day. He didn't want to. He brought his friends with him so that he wouldn't have to talk to you. And he told me that although the headmaster begged your sisters to come too, they all refused.'

I began to cry, but he ignored my tears and carried on talking, in a pseudo-sympathetic voice. 'The school sent letters to both your parents too,' he said. 'But neither of them even bothered to answer.' He stood up, walked towards the open door and, turning to look at me with an expression of spiteful triumph, said, 'I'm the only one who loves you.' Then he left the room, closing the door behind him.

I cried myself to sleep that night, silently so that none of the other boys would hear me, and I was still asleep when Johnson came for me, lifted me out of my bed and carried me up to the top floor. He put me down on a pile of sheets in the corner of the art room and started talking about my family again. He seemed to know exactly where to dig the knife in to cause me maximum pain, and then he twisted it mercilessly.

The nuns had instilled in me the belief that no one loved or wanted me, and Johnson had continued the process they'd started of destroying my confidence and sense of self-worth – or what remained of it by the time

I went to Knossington Grange. I'd always believed that what they all said was true, because, for as long as I could remember, I'd always been alone. So when I'd seen my brother in the school grounds earlier that day, it had felt as though there was a chance they'd been wrong and that I *did* have someone who cared about me. But what Johnson was telling me made me realise I'd been fooling myself: nothing had changed, nobody cared, and I *was* all alone.

As Johnson talked, he stroked my head, and then suddenly said, 'Call me Daddy. If you call me Daddy, everything will be all right.' I tried to turn away from him, but he held my head firmly in his hands and kept repeating 'Just call me Daddy,' until eventually, between my sobs, I whispered the word 'Daddy', and then he raped me.

When he'd finished, he handed me a roll-up and a beer and I smoked the cigarette and drank from the can without even being aware of what I was doing. I knew that this was the way things were always going to be from now on and I felt defeated. What did it matter anyway? All I needed to do was find a way to retain the numb feeling I had at that moment and stop caring about stupid, waste-of-time things like being loved. I'd been dealt my hand and I just had to stop complaining and accept it.

One day, during school, our teacher took us to the nearby graveyard to do some grave rubbings. It was never a good idea to let anyone know when you were upset about anything – the boys at Knossington Grange weren't the sort who would sympathise and try to cheer you up. But I found it difficult to hide the fact that being in the graveyard unnerved me and made me feel anxious. I still had nightmares and flashbacks of the night when the nuns had threatened to bury me alive in the graveyard at Nazareth House, and while all the other boys were making jokes and doing grave rubbings, I started to have a panic attack.

I was sitting on the lawn facing the school building and trying to breathe when Mr Johnson walked across the grass towards me. He must have seen me from a window and realised that I was upset. He sat down beside me and asked what was bothering me. I suppose I needed to talk about it – and I wasn't exactly spoilt for choice when it came to finding a sympathetic ear – so I told him. Crying and barely coherent, I described how the nuns had dragged me out of my bed and held me above an open grave until I was so frightened I thought my heart was going to stop beating, and how they'd dropped me into it and I'd really believed they were going to bury me alive.

Mr Johnson was clearly shocked by what he could understand of what I was saying. But when I'd finished telling him about the worst thing that had ever happened to me in my short lifetime of horrible experiences, he asked what I'd done to deserve such a punishment.

'Nothing,' I told him. 'What *could* anyone do to deserve that?'

He laughed and insisted, 'You must have done something. They must have had a good reason to do something like that.' Then he sighed, slapped his hands against his thighs and said, 'Well, it just goes to confirm what I've already told you: I'm the only person in the world who loves you.'

It felt as though an insect was crawling down my spine. Whether or not Mr Johnson 'loved' me was open to debate, but what I did know at that moment, with absolute certainty, was that he was the only person I really needed to fear and that I might just have made a terrible mistake.

I was still fighting with other boys, and getting into trouble for it, as well as for the confrontations I often had with teachers and other members of staff at the school. But I wasn't really afraid of anyone else. Even when I was taking a beating from an older boy and was in the throes of trying – and failing – to defend myself, I wasn't scared. My nose might be bleeding and my body might be bruised, but my anger made me insensitive to the pain and I was never frightened for my life. It was only Mr Johnson who made me feel that way.

I can't think now what could possibly have made me tell him about my worst and most terrible fear, except that he caught me with my guard down, because being in the graveyard at school that day had made me vulnerable. Telling him was a stupid thing to do, and I might have known he'd use the information I'd given him against me.

After that day, he'd often say to me when I was misbehaving, 'If you don't stop that immediately, I'll take you to the graveyard,' or 'I'll dig a grave for you if you carry on like that.' I'd feel sick with foreboding and would immediately stop whatever it was I was doing wrong.

Then, one night, as Johnson was waking me up, I threw a punch, which hit him in the face. It wasn't deliberate – I may have been a disturbed child, but I wasn't a stupid one and I'd never have dared try to fight with him; it was just an instinctive reaction because I was half asleep and taken by surprise.

He didn't say anything, but I could feel his anger when he put his hand over my mouth and lifted me out of bed. He'd only ever taken me up the stairs before that night, and as soon as I realised we were going down them, I began to feel even more anxious than usual.

By the time he'd carried me out of the building, through the car park and up the hill above the woods, I was panicking. I began to struggle and tried to twist my body so that he would be forced to put me down. But he was strong and he could hold me easily, even with one hand still clamped firmly over my mouth.

When we reached the graveyard, I was sobbing, and as

I pressed my face against Johnson's chest, the fear inside me kept growing until it had blocked out all other thoughts and feelings.

'Which grave would you like to be buried in?' Johnson asked me, and when I begged him to take me back to my room, he threw back his head and laughed with genuine amusement. He was still laughing when he bent down and laid me on one of the graves, so that my head was touching the gravestone. I'd stopped sobbing by that time, because the fear inside me had grown so huge I couldn't breathe.

Suddenly, Johnson's mood changed and although he continued to laugh, he started punching me in the stomach, over and over again, until I vomited. Then he grabbed a fistful of my hair and pulled me off the gravestone and across the grass. He paused beside another grave and pushed my face up against the grey roughness of its tombstone. Then he took me to another and another, until finally he dropped me on the ground and sat down beside me.

He rolled a cigarette and leaned back against a gravestone to smoke it, while I lay silently on the grass, paralysed by a dread that my mind couldn't process.

After a few minutes, Johnson stood up, lifted me into his arms and carried me back to school, where he took me to the bathroom, removed my pyjamas and washed the sour-smelling soil off my body. Later, as he tucked me into bed, he bent down, looked directly into my eyes and said, 'You're mine.' Then he walked out of the room and closed the door behind him.

Even on the nights when I wasn't woken up by Johnson, I didn't sleep well. I knew I was even more vulnerable when I was asleep, so I'd try to keep myself awake for as long as possible and when my eyes did eventually close, I'd have nightmares, from which I'd wake up screaming and drenched in sweat. Inevitably, I was finding it increasingly difficult to concentrate in school, so I wasn't really learning anything at all. I was short-tempered too, which meant I was getting into more fights and was constantly in trouble, both in and out of the classroom.

It felt as though something was building up inside me – some sort of negative energy – and every time I snapped at someone or lashed out with my fists, I'd release a bit of it. But it was never long before what I'd lost had been replaced – and added to – and then the whole process would start all over again.

I wasn't really aware of how bad things were, though, until the day I got into a fight with a boy in the courtyard and by the time a teacher dragged me off him, I'd almost strangled him. Although I'd been totally unaware of what I was doing, I'd been banging his head repeatedly on the ground, and it shocked me when I realised I'd completely lost it. When I was angry, I didn't seem to have any control over my actions – and that scared me.

The school had a resident psychologist, whose professional services we were all in need of to some degree or another. He was a nice enough man, who used to wear jeans, T-shirts and trainers in what I think was an attempt to fit in with the boys and make us feel that he was one of us. Perhaps it worked with some of the boys, because I know there were some who opened up and told him things. But although there were very few things in my life I was sure about between the ages of twelve and fourteen, one of them was the knowledge that it would be a very serious mistake ever to tell anyone anything about myself. I'd known that before I'd told Mr Johnson about what the nuns had done to me in the graveyard at Nazareth House, and I'd paid the consequences of letting my guard slip because I was upset. But it wasn't going to happen again.

We had weekly classes with the psychologist, when he'd make us sit on the floor in a circle and play 'games'. Looking back on it now, I suppose they were all about trust and empathy and trying to make us open up and talk about our fears – which might have seemed like a good idea from *his* point of view. However, it didn't take very much imagination to realise that, in a school like Knossington Grange, telling other boys that you were afraid at all, let alone describing your fears to them, was only going to add to your problems. We all had our own emotional, behavioural and developmental issues and, despite the psychologist's best efforts, sympathy and understanding remained in fairly short supply.

Surprisingly though, some of the boys did open up – and subsequently paid the price for their naivety. But I always kept my mouth firmly shut, both in and out of those classes. So the psychologist started giving me one-to-one sessions, during which he tried to hypnotise me.

He wanted to fix my stammer and I know he meant well. So, although it didn't work, I was grateful to him for bothering to try. I imagine that for hypnosis to succeed however, it has to be done by someone you trust, and the chances of my trusting *anyone*, let alone a man I barely knew, were slim to non-existent. Quite apart from my fear of what might happen to me while I was hypnotised, I was afraid of revealing something about myself that might make me vulnerable or that might expose something about me that I'd rather no one knew – or, indeed, something I'd rather not know myself, such as that I really was the Devil's child.

On the morning of my thirteenth birthday, I woke up to find a balloon tied to the end of my bed. Beside it were a bag of sweets, a smiley-face mug and a badge. I knew that they were gifts from Mr Johnson – he always gave the same things to all the boys under his direct care on their birthdays. The problem was that I hated birth-days. I hadn't ever had one that I'd enjoyed, so I'd learned to ignore them and treat them like any other day.

Mr Johnson came into the bedroom while we were getting ready for school, handed me an envelope and said, 'Go on, open it.' He was grinning like an idiot and he stroked my hair as I read the words on his pathetic card – which I knew was the only card I'd get that day. I'd long ago stopped receiving birthday cards and £5 notes from 'your loving Mammy', and I'd almost managed to convince myself I didn't care.

I pulled away from Mr Johnson's hand on my head, but he continued to smile his falsely jovial smile as he said, in what I imagined might be a proud father's sort of voice, 'Well, you're a teenager now!' Then he added, in a quieter, almost threatening tone, 'I've got more presents for you. I'll see you after school.' And he left the room.

As soon as he'd gone, I threw the bag of sweets on to the floor, tossed his card into the bin and went into the bathroom, where I smashed the stupid smiley mug against the tiles.

At break time that morning, I was standing in the courtyard when Mr Johnson walked towards me and surreptitiously handed me a can of beer, which I shared with a couple of other boys in the woods when we went there to smoke our cigarettes.

I went up to my room after school and found Mr Johnson standing beside my bed. He asked me if I was having a nice birthday, and when I nodded, he said, 'Well, you don't look as though you're enjoying it. I'll have to do something special for you later to cheer you up.' He gave a bark of laughter as he walked out of the room, and I sat down on my bed to wait for my heart to stop banging against my ribs and for the feeling of nausea to pass.

I tried to avoid him that evening. But, as if the fates were reminding me that I wasn't the one who was in charge, I probably bumped into him more than usual. And every time I saw him, he smirked at me as though we were co-conspirators in some eagerly anticipated plot, until I knew I couldn't face whatever he had in store for me, and I decided to run away.

# Chapter Eleven

After supper, I slipped out of school and into the woods, where I sat under a tree in the darkening evening light and smoked a cigarette. I was still racking my brains trying to think of somewhere I could go when the heavens opened and, within seconds, I was soaked to the skin.

I lifted my head, turned my face towards the rain and swore loudly at the sky. Nothing ever seemed to go right for me. The ground around me was already turning to mud, and I knew there was no point trying to run away during a rainstorm in the dark. So, still shouting and swearing, I ran back into the school building and sat in the changing room, shivering and dripping water on to the floor while I smoked another cigarette and tried not to think about what lay ahead of me that night.

I was still crouched on one of the metal lockers, cigarette in hand, when a teacher came into the room and sent me to join my group, who were watching television. I stopped outside the door of the lounge, closed my eyes and took a deep breath, and as I walked into the room, Mr Johnson greeted me with exaggerated delight. Almost pushing the boy who was sitting on his knee on to the floor, he announced that 'the place of honour' was mine, because it was my birthday and I'd just become a teenager. When I hesitated, he reached out and grabbed my arm. But I only sat on his knee for a few minutes before I stammered something about needing to go to the toilet and left the room.

I tried to stay awake that night, and as I lay in bed, with my eyes wide open and tears dampening the pillow under my head, I prayed silently to anyone who might be able to hear me. But I was asleep when Johnson came for me.

As he was carrying me up the stairs to the staff quarters on the top floor, we heard footsteps on the landing just above us. He gave me a warning look and darted into the toilet, where he put me down on the floor, held his finger to his lips and mouthed at me, 'I'll kill you.' Then he opened the door and stepped out on to the landing.

I could hear the muffled voice of the woman who looked after us on Johnson's evenings off. Then I heard Johnson laugh and say, 'Goodnight.' For a moment, I thought about calling out for help. But even if I hadn't been so afraid and so certain that Johnson really would kill me if

I did, it was already too late. The door of the toilet opened and he stepped inside, locking it behind him before putting his hand over my mouth and whispering into my ear, 'I swear I'll kill you if you make a sound.'

I had a sudden, almost overwhelming urge to sink my teeth into the palm of his hand and scream. But what was the point? Whatever I did, Johnson would make up some excuse to explain the inexplicable fact of being in the toilet in the middle of the night with one of the children he was employed to take care of. And I knew that whatever he said, however unlikely it might sound, no one was going to believe me instead of him.

So I didn't bite his hand and I didn't scream, and after a while he opened the door, picked me up and carried me along the corridor to his room.

Johnson's bedroom smelt of booze, tobacco and sweat. It was untidy and its only furniture was a single bed, a wardrobe and an armchair, which was placed squarely in front of the television. He put me down on the bed, picked up a can of beer from the stack on the floor and handed it to me. I shook my head, but he twisted his fingers into my hair and poured it down my throat. Then he opened another can and did the same thing, and by the time the second one was empty, the room had started to spin.

I felt sick. My limbs were heavy, but my head felt as though it was floating above my shoulders, and it took me a few seconds to identify the sound I could hear as being someone knocking on the door. Although my eyes wouldn't focus properly, it looked as though the handle . . . and that was the moment when Johnson almost threw himself across the room.

Slamming his foot against the door, he opened it just a couple of inches and stood so that the bulk of his large body was blocking the person's view into the room. I heard a woman's voice and when Johnson spoke he sounded irritated. Then he closed the door and turned the key in the lock.

After he'd removed my clothes and then his own, he started taking pictures of me with a Polaroid camera. I told him I felt sick, but he didn't answer; he just kept snapping away with his camera and arranging my body in different positions, almost as though I was an inanimate model rather than a real person – and a child.

I must have blacked out, because the next thing I knew we were in the art room and I was lying on a mattress, without any memory of how I'd got there. I tried to stand up, but Johnson punched me in the stomach, and as all the air rushed out of my body, he pushed a piece of material into my mouth, put his hands around my neck and pressed his thumbs against my windpipe. I was still fighting for breath when he hung me up by the neck from the wooden post, laughing when I kicked out wildly with my legs and waved my arms in the air as I searched in vain for something to hold on to.

Later, after he'd raped me and taken more photographs, I lay on the mattress and he sat down beside me to roll a cigarette. When he'd smoked it, he carried me down the stairs, bent over me as he placed me on my bed and whispered again, 'Keep your mouth shut, or I'll kill you.'

The next morning in assembly, the headmaster talked about problems – how everyone has them and how we shouldn't keep them bottled up inside us. He reminded us that his door was always open and that we could talk to him about anything. He'd said the same thing many times before, but this time it seemed almost as though he was speaking directly to me, and I decided to tell him about Mr Johnson.

There were other boys waiting to see Mr Smith when I went to his office later that morning, so I joined the queue and I was still standing there when I saw Mr Johnson walking towards us. He paused beside me just long enough to say, 'I've been looking for you. Your room is like a pigsty. Get upstairs immediately and clean it up.' Then he continued to walk down the corridor towards the stairs.

There was no point in arguing. I stepped out of the queue and followed him, and as soon as we were inside my room, he shut the door and demanded to know why I'd been standing outside the headmaster's office.

'I'm going to tell him,' I said. I felt a sudden surge of courage and I looked up into his face defiantly as I added, 'I'm going to tell Mr Smith what you've been doing to me.'

Mr Johnson laughed and, fastening his fingers tightly around my throat, lifted me off the ground and hissed at me with angry malice, 'And do you really think he's going to believe you? Do you think anyone would believe a trouble-maker like you instead of a man like me?' Then, in case I hadn't already appreciated the futility of what I'd been planning to do, he added, almost conversationally, 'Would you like to pay another little visit to the graveyard?' And this time when he laughed, his amusement seemed genuine. He released his grip around my throat so abruptly that I banged my hip painfully on the side of the bed as I dropped to the floor, which is where I was still lying when he strode out of the room, slamming the door behind him.

I didn't go back to join the line of boys with problems who were waiting to talk to the headmaster. But Mr Johnson must have been at least a bit worried by what I'd threatened to do, because he came to find me later that day and gave me cigarettes and money, patting me on the back as he promised to give me more if I kept my mouth shut.

After lunch, I was walking across the playground when

Mr Smith came striding towards me and, without giving myself time to think, I blurted out, 'Mr Johnson's hurting me, sir.'

The headmaster blinked at me, as if he was trying to remember who I was, and then he touched his head absent-mindedly as I added quickly, 'I mean he's *really* hurting me. And because you said that if we had a problem we could talk to you, I want to talk to you about what Mr Johnson's doing.'

Unfortunately though, the words didn't come out quite like that, because I was stuttering, so bits of them got stuck under my tongue. And maybe Mr Smith didn't understand what I was trying to say, because he frowned at me and said, 'Don't be silly, boy. Get back to your classroom.' Or maybe it was just that being sexually abused by your housemaster wasn't the sort of problem he'd meant us to share with him.

After school, I was sitting on my bed when the door burst open and Mr Johnson stormed into the bedroom, swiped me across the head with the back of his hand so hard that I fell on to the floor, and shouted at the two other boys who were in there to get out. They didn't need telling twice and as they almost fell over each other in their haste to comply, Mr Johnson slammed the door shut behind them.

I'd just got to my feet when he turned back towards

me and smacked me across the head again. I'd often seen him angry, but never before in such a raging fury. His face was red as he spat at me, 'What the fuck have you been doing? Didn't I warn you that I'd kill you if you opened your mouth? And now the headmaster tells me you've been complaining about me. Surely that can't be right.' He grabbed my hair, yanking my head sharply backwards so that I was forced to look at him as he shouted, 'Can it?'

'It doesn't matter anyway,' I told him, stuttering and raising my arm in front of my face in an automatic gesture of self-protection. 'Smith didn't want to know. So you're in the clear.' But Mr Johnson didn't say anything; he just hit me again and then walked out of the room.

That night, I tried to keep the other boys in my room awake, but within minutes of lights out I knew I was the only one still lying with my eyes open in the dark. I hated the waiting. My whole body was drenched in sweat and eventually, with my heart thumping, I got up and crawled underneath my bed, which is where I was lying, asleep, when Johnson came for me.

He dragged me up off the floor, put one hand over my mouth and carried me out of the room, down the stairs, through the front door and the car park and into the woods. That alone was enough to frighten me almost out of my wits, but there was something about Johnson that night that made me believe he was going to carry out the threat he'd made so often and kill me.

As soon as we were far enough into the woods not to be seen from the school, he put me down on the ground, removed my pyjamas and told me to kneel with the palms of my hands together and my head bowed. Then, as he walked round me slowly, he said, in a cold, menacing voice, 'Pray to me while I'm deciding what to do with you.'

'Please don't hurt me,' I whispered. 'I'm sorry. I don't know why I said anything to Mr Smith. But he didn't believe me anyway. I won't do it again. I promise. I'm sorry.'

'I can't hear you,' Johnson said. 'You'll have to say it again. And this time at least try to sound as though you mean it.'

'I'm sorry,' I said again, more loudly.

Johnson laid a rucksack on the ground beside me and pulled out a roll of tape. As he tore off a length of it, it made a sudden, sharp ripping sound, which seemed to ricochet off the trees. He pressed the piece of tape against my mouth and when he reached out his hands towards me again, I cowered away from him and he laughed. Pushing my arms down by my sides, he taped them to my body, before pulling me up so that I was standing, bound and shivering, in front of him.

As he reached into the rucksack again, he seemed to be detached from what he was doing, almost as though he was in a trance. He pulled out a thick coil of rope, tied one end of it around my ankles and tried to throw the other end over the branch of a tree above our heads. But each time he threw it, he missed and swore angrily before trying again, until, eventually, the rope curled around the branch and its loose end dropped back to the ground at his feet.

Johnson glanced towards me and began to pull on the end of the rope, lifting me slowly off the ground until my upside-down head was just inches from his face. Then he tied the loose end to a low branch and began to swing me backwards and forwards. As the blood filled my ears and pounded inside my head, I had a sudden terrifying thought. What if he left me hanging there until my head was so full of blood it began to seep out of my body? Or what if the rope snapped or the knots worked themselves loose, so that I fell and smashed my skull on the ground?

Johnson stood beside me, laughing into my face, and then he untied the end of the rope and lowered me to the ground. I was very cold and very frightened and the skin around my ankles was burning. But I felt an overwhelming sense of relief at the thought that Johnson had had his fun and I'd survived my punishment for daring to open my mouth. I should have known better.

As I lay on the damp ground, Johnson untied the rope from around my ankles and re-tied it around my neck, asking me as he did so, 'Are you sorry?' When I nodded mutely, he put his mouth close to my ear and whispered, 'Liar.' Then he tugged on the rope and I felt a searing-hot pain in my neck. I couldn't struggle, because my arms were still taped to my sides, but I kicked out with my legs, which only made the rope tighten around my throat so that I began to choke.

Johnson took the weight of my body in his arms for a moment and then he let go of me again, put a torch on the ground underneath me, like a spotlight, and took a photograph. When he turned the torch off, it seemed that the woods were darker than they'd been before, and I was suddenly even more afraid.

Johnson started dancing around me like a crazed Morris dancer, pausing occasionally to take the weight of my body for a few seconds, so that I could gasp for air, and then swinging me backwards and forwards a few times until it felt as though my neck was going to snap in two. I thought I was going to die, but when he began to whip me and sexually assault me, that fear became a wish.

By the time he untied me and dropped me on the ground, my mind was completely numb. Although I hadn't died, something inside me – whatever it was that made me feel like *me* – had been killed, and I didn't even have the energy to cry.

Johnson sat beside me, resting his back casually against a tree as he rolled a cigarette, lit it and handed it to me. He was smiling the triumphant smile of the victor as he said, '*Now* do you understand that you're mine? *I* decide what happens to you, nobody else. Nobody cares about you except me. You know I'm right, don't you?'

And I nodded, because I knew he was.

After Johnson had dressed me in my pyjamas and carried me back to my room, I fell into a deep, exhausted, nightmare-haunted sleep, and when I woke up screaming, he was standing by my bed. For a moment, I felt disorientated and confused. Had I imagined I'd been asleep? Had he only just put me down on the bed? And then I realised it was morning and the other boys were already bumbling around the room getting dressed.

I started to sit up, but Johnson pushed my shoulders back on to the pillow and slid one of his hands under the bedclothes and inside my pyjamas. Then he squeezed my private parts as he said, 'Mine. Anytime I want it. Okay?' And, again, I nodded my head.

When I woke up that day, I felt as though something had snapped inside me and I simply couldn't take any more. I knew I couldn't do anything to stop what Johnson was doing to me, which meant I *had* to find some way of dealing with it. So the next time Johnson came for me in the night, I visualised my sister Geraldine lifting me on to her knee, wrapping her arms tightly around me and, with her chin resting lightly on the top of my head, talking to me in her calm, soothing voice and telling me stories about animals that could talk or knights in shining armour who fought battles on the side of good against evil. I imagined, too, that as long as my mind was with Geraldine, my body was just an empty paper bag – and if I wasn't inside it, it didn't matter what Johnson did to it.

Separating my mind and body seemed to work, because although what Johnson did to me still hurt, it was as though he was no longer really doing it to *me*. And as well as helping me to detach myself just a little bit from what was happening, that also gave me a sense of satisfaction, because it felt as though I'd scored a secret victory over him, which had reduced the power he held over me – even if only by an almost immeasurably small amount.

I was fourteen in 1979, when the FA Cup final took place between Arsenal and Manchester United. All the boys at school watched the match – the seniors on one television and the juniors and middle group, with Mr Johnson, on another. Because Mr Johnson was an Arsenal fan, we supported them too, while the seniors rooted loudly for Manchester United. Every time a team scored a goal, its supporters would run across the room to where the other group was sitting to jump up and down while cheering at the top of their lungs. It was all very good-humoured and good fun, which was quite an achievement, considering the fact that several of the boys were prone to losing their tempers at the slightest provocation.

When the match ended – in a 3–2 win to Arsenal – Mr Johnson announced that he was taking the boy who was 'the only true Arsenal fan amongst you all' to his room to give him some sweets. The boy was crimson with embarrassment as he followed Mr Johnson out of the room, and as soon as the door closed behind them, the senior boys started sniggering. They called Mr Johnson 'a fucking kiddie fiddler' and 'a queer', which is when I realised that, whatever happened, I must do everything and anything in my power to make sure none of the other boys ever found out what he'd done to me.

I suppose the thing about getting away with doing something wrong is that the longer someone manages to do it, the more they're inclined to believe they're untouchable and that normal rules of morality or criminality don't apply to them. And I think that was what was happening with Johnson.

It wasn't only the boys who were talking about him: it was becoming clear that members of staff were finding his behaviour difficult to deal with too, particularly as he became less able to hide the fact that he was drinking heavily. And when the boys sensed that he was losing the whole-hearted support of other teachers, they began to voice their own feelings about him more openly – although anyone who said anything derogatory about him within earshot of a member of staff was still rounded on and told, in no uncertain terms, to shut up.

Then, one day, a rumour began to spread amongst the boys that Johnson was in the headmaster's office and the two men were shouting at each other because Mr Smith had confronted Johnson about his drinking and had told him that some of the boys had raised complaints about his behaviour. We were all still talking excitedly about what we'd heard when the first rumour was eclipsed by another – that Mr Smith had dismissed Johnson on the spot for sexual abuse.

I didn't believe the second story, about Johnson getting the sack – at least not until I saw him loading suitcases into his car. After I'd stood and watched him silently for a while, I shouted at him angrily, 'One day you'll pay for what you've done.' But he just looked at me as though he'd only just noticed me standing there, then he laughed and strode back into the school to collect more of his belongings.

I was still standing there when he got into his car and I watched him drive out of the school gates. It felt as though the heavy weight that had always been in my stomach since shortly after I'd started at the school was evaporating. I wasn't looking forward to the arrival of the police and all their questions – I dreaded the thought of having to admit I'd been one of the boys Johnson had been abusing. But he deserved to be punished for what he'd done and I *was* looking forward to knowing that justice was going to be served at last. What mattered most of all, though, was the fact that Johnson had gone and his reign of evil abuse was over.

As each day passed and there was still no sign of the police, I became increasingly anxious. Although neither Mr Smith nor any of the teachers mentioned Johnson's name at all, the boys talked about little else, and they turned, like a pack of wolves, on those who were unlucky enough to have been known to be Johnson's favourites.

As the weight settled in my stomach again, I kept expecting someone to point the finger at me. But, gradually, it dawned on me that no one knew I was one of what had become known as 'Johnson's bum boys'. And as I certainly wasn't going to volunteer the information, it started to look as though I might be able to avoid being exposed.

I watched as Johnson's favourites were chased into the woods, taunted and beaten up. It seemed grossly unfair to blame them for the terrible abuse they'd been subjected to, and I felt sorry for them. I knew that some of the boys doing the chasing had also been Johnson's victims, and I can only assume that they were as deeply ashamed of themselves as I was of myself when I joined in some of the beatings in the same hope of hiding the fact that I, too, had been abused by him.

Becoming a hunter instead of the hunted was a simple matter of self-preservation. You don't have to be a master-mind to realise that a school full of maladjusted boys isn't the place to expose your weaknesses or admit to having done anything – however reluctantly – that could make you the victim of bullying. I had a reputation at the school for being able to take care of myself, and although there was a whole world of difference between punching some boy who tried to bully me and defending myself against a fully grown man who was manipulating my already damaged emotions and threatening – very convincingly – to kill me if I didn't do what he told me to do, I was pretty sure the other boys wouldn't see the distinction. So I felt as though I had no choice other than to join in the chasing and the attacks and just live with the fact that I had yet another reason to hate myself.

As the days became weeks and still no one asked any questions about Johnson, everyone gradually lost interest in talking about him, and although I was relieved at the thought that I'd escaped being identified as one of his victims, it also meant that he wasn't going to be called to account for what he'd done. I realised that he was going to get away with it, and the anger built up inside me until I was barely able to control it.

Now that he'd left the school, I could at least go to sleep every night safe in the knowledge that no one was going to creep into my bedroom and carry me upstairs. But I was having terrible nightmares. Almost every night, I'd wake up in a cold sweat with my heart thudding, and it would be several seconds or more before I knew where I was and remembered that Johnson had gone. As a result, I was tired all the time and I was still constantly anxious.

I'd lost the plot as far as school was concerned too. I spent most of my time in class provoking fights and being disruptive, doing stupid things that were guaranteed to get me into trouble. Perhaps I wanted to be punished. The events of my childhood had made me vulnerable, and Johnson had recognised and used my emotional fragility to his advantage, deliberately alternating between trying to win my affection so that I felt dependent on him and frightening and threatening me to establish his control. And although I knew there was nothing I could have done to stop him abusing me, I still felt guilty.

As time passed, it was sometimes difficult to remember how helpless, frightened and profoundly miserable he'd made me feel – although I could always evoke those emotions very clearly in my nightmares. By a combination of mental and physical abuse, he'd stripped away what remained of my self-confidence and, with it, any ability I might otherwise have had of fighting back against him. Now that he'd gone, though, I felt as though I'd been weak and that it was somehow my fault he'd abused me. As the nightmares continued to wear me down, I often wished Johnson *had* killed me when he'd hung me by the neck and I'd thought that dying was the worst thing that could happen to me.

By picking fights with other – mostly older, bigger – boys and being beaten up, it was as though I was getting some of the punishment I thought I deserved. It was like self-harming by proxy, and sometimes, having thrown the first punch, I'd just stand there, making no attempt to defend myself as the boy I'd attacked for no apparent reason did his best to beat me to a pulp.

One of the boys at school had access to cannabis and I began to beg, borrow and steal money to buy as much of it as I could. I'd smoke a joint and wait for the critical moment when enough of it had built up in my system to start slowly washing away the pain, leaving me suspended in a dreamlike world where nothing could reach me. And if nothing could reach me, nothing could hurt me. The problem was that I didn't get on with the boy who was supplying the cannabis, and one day, after we'd had yet another fight, he refused to sell any more to me.

As soon as I stopped smoking it, the pain, the nightmares and the urge to kill myself all came flooding back, until eventually it reached the point when I couldn't think about anything except how bad I felt. Then, one night, I pulled the cord off my dressing gown and went out into the woods at the front of the school, where I knew no one would be able to see me.

The dark trees looked sinister and threatening in the dim moonlight, but I was barely aware of my surroundings as I climbed up one of them and tied one end of the cord around my neck and the other to a thick branch above my head. As I sat there, willing myself to jump and hating myself for being too pathetic to do it, I began to make a list in my head of all the reasons not to kill myself. Even including the ones that weren't really reasons at all, it was a very short list. But still I couldn't find the courage to jump.

I crouched on the branch and cried – because I was lonely and miserable, because everything in my life was hopeless, and because, however hard I tried, I couldn't see anything good in the future that lay ahead of me. I was still berating myself for being weak and pathetic when the branch below my feet creaked and then, with a loud, echoing 'crack', snapped in two at exactly the same moment as I felt an excruciating pain in my neck.

Maybe I slipped – as I thought I'd done when I tried to hang myself at Nazareth House – or maybe I did jump. I'll never know the truth. But as I hung there, waiting to die, it slowly dawned on me that although the rope was burning my neck, I was still breathing. Clearly, I'd done something wrong when I'd tied the knot, and as I raised my hand to touch it, it suddenly unravelled and I fell to the ground with a thud.

I hurt my leg when I landed, and I was lying under the trees, clutching it against my chest and swearing, when I heard a voice in my head say, 'You failed. You never get anything right.' And although I was angry with myself because I knew what the voice had said was true, it didn't really matter, because I knew, too, that one day I would succeed.

# Chapter Twelve

After Johnson had left and things at school had settled into a sort of normality, and as my hormones raged like those of any other teenage boy, my thoughts turned to girls.

One Saturday, I went into the local town of Oakham and met a really nice girl called Susie. It was four miles to Oakham, but it wasn't long before I was walking there every day after school to see her. We went on long walks together and talked about everything and anything; or we'd go to the cinema, although I couldn't have told anyone the plot of any of the films we were supposed to be watching, because we were too busy kissing in the back row to pay any attention to what was happening on the screen. Afterwards, I'd walk the four miles back to Knossington Grange, thinking about Susie and about how extraordinary it felt to know that someone actually cared about me at last.

It wasn't long, though, before some of the local lads became aware that a boy from Knossington Grange was seeing one of 'their' girls, and one evening, as I was walking back to school in the dark, I was ambushed by some of them. I was taken completely by surprise, so I didn't get the chance to fight back as they punched and kicked me from all angles and then told me to clear off and not go back to Oakham again.

The next evening, I was approaching the town at the usual time when I saw two of the lads who'd attacked me the previous night. They hadn't yet seen me, so I bent down quickly, picked up a piece of wood and then ducked behind a wall out of sight. I waited, listening to their voices getting louder as they came closer to where I was hiding, and when they were directly in line with the wall, I jumped out and whacked the nearest lad with the bit of wood. He fell to the ground like a sack of potatoes, and before I even had a chance to turn round, his mate was already legging it back towards town.

As the boy I'd hit sat on the ground rubbing the side of his head, I told him, 'This may be your town, but I'm going to keep coming here whenever I want.' He glanced at me quickly as he got to his feet and, staggering slightly, raised his arm in front of his face, presumably in anticipation of me whacking him again. But I didn't want to fight anyone; I'd just been making a point. So I took a step away from him to give him space, and he stumbled off down the road, back towards town.

I didn't say anything to Susie about what had happened, because I didn't want to upset her. But I knew the fight wasn't over, and I was ready for the reception committee that was waiting for me later that evening as I walked out of town and along the usually deserted lane towards school. They were ahead of me on the road, watching me walk towards them, and as soon as I saw them, I started scanning the ditch for a suitable weapon. Almost without breaking my stride, I grabbed a thick piece of wood, about a foot long, from the side of the road and held it tightly in the hand that I let drop, casually, at my side.

There were four of them, and although I tried to look mean and fearless, my stomach was churning. When I was still a few feet away from them, I stopped walking and shouted, 'Come on then. Who's fucking first?' One of them laughed and stepped forward, and I swung the piece of wood, striking him so hard on the side of the head that I sent him flying through the air.

I turned round immediately to face the other three, ready for the onslaught. But none of them moved, and they were still just standing watching me when I walked past them and disappeared into the darkness.

I'd been walking for about fifteen minutes when I heard the sound of a motorbike behind me. But before I'd had time to react, I was lying in a ditch at the side of the road with a blinding pain in my head. Whatever the pillion rider had hit me with nearly cracked my skull, but anger can make you stubborn, and there was no way I was going to back down. Although the odds weren't good, at four against one, I did have one significant advantage: whereas they were just annoyed because an outsider from a school for boys with 'social and behavioural problems' was seeing one of 'their' girls, I had a whole lifetime of suppressed rage, frustration and unhappiness all coiled up inside me, just waiting for an excuse to burst out.

I knew that the next time we bumped into each other, I'd need a weapon. So, before I left school the following afternoon, I sneaked into the kitchen and helped myself to a small fruit knife, which I taped to my leg under my jeans.

I was waiting outside the cinema for Susie when I saw them walking towards me. I didn't have time to bend down and get the knife before the largest of the four lads was standing right in front of me. He was a good few inches taller than I was, and he bent down slightly so that our faces were on a level as he said, 'You're fucking mental. You're just going to keep coming, aren't you?'

'Every day, mate,' I answered, looking him squarely in the eyes. 'Every day.'

Suddenly he laughed and held out his hand, so I shook

it. The next time I saw him in Oakham, he grinned and gave me the thumbs up, and I grinned back at him, because it felt as though, for the first time in my life, I'd earned someone else's respect.

When I was nearly sixteen and my time at Knossington Grange was coming to an end, I began to think about what I was going to do next. Things had got better for me at school after Johnson had gone, but I was still looking forward to the prospect of leaving and going back to Nottingham to live. The one thing I would miss was Susie.

I'd passed just one exam – to gain a CSE in maths – and I knew that my almost complete lack of any educational achievements meant that prospective employers wouldn't exactly be falling over themselves to sign me up to work for them. As ever, my fate was in the hands of Social Services, and my social worker sent me to see a careers adviser who specialised in dealing with people 'like me' – i.e. people with problems and no qualifications.

The careers adviser seemed earnest enough, and he was probably the only person who'd ever asked me what I actually *wanted* to do. But when I answered, 'I want to be a social worker,' he looked up so quickly from the papers on his desk that his glasses nearly slid off the end of his nose, and there was no doubting the incredulity in his voice as he repeated, 'You want to be a social worker?'

'Yes,' I said, half expecting to be able to hear the sound of my already fragile confidence finally shattering like broken glass.

'Well. Hmm.' He cleared his throat, pushed his glasses back up his nose and leaned across his desk towards me. 'Listen, lad, I'm afraid you'd need a rather better educational record than you've got, and you'd have to study for four years to become a social worker.' He smiled ruefully and shrugged his shoulders.

'You asked me what I wanted to do,' I told him. 'Well, that's what I want to do, and I'm prepared to study to do it.' I tried to laugh as I added, 'After all, I've already got a pretty good understanding of the care system and how it works.'

He was clearly trying to look interested and sympathetic, but he couldn't hide his impatience as he explained that although it was commendable to have aspirations, mine were unrealistic in the extreme, as were any ideas I might have of doing any sort of further education at all. Then he offered me an opportunity to learn picture framing and, because I know when I'm beating my head against a brick wall, I agreed to go for an interview.

The careers adviser went with me to talk to the manager of the picture-framing company, and he accepted the job I was offered on my behalf. Afterwards, he beamed at me as though I'd done something highly commendable. But although I tried to tell myself that getting work of any sort was an achievement, it wasn't what I wanted to do. It felt as though my life had already been mapped out for me – and as I'd never been given any choice about anything that had happened to me in the last sixteen years, I don't know why I'd thought things might be different once I left school.

Back at Knossington Grange, Mr Smith congratulated me on getting the job, and when I told him it wasn't really what I wanted to do, he shrugged his shoulders and said, 'Beggars can't be choosers' – which seemed to be as true as it was depressing.

A few days after the job interview, my social worker came to see me to tell me about a youth hostel in Nottingham specifically for boys coming out of the care system. A week later, she took me to a big house in a rough area of town, which was conveniently situated next door to a police station. I didn't trust anyone, but the manager seemed a nice enough man and he said he'd be happy for me to move in.

Before I left school for good, I spent my last evening with Susie. We cried and promised to stay in touch – although I think both of us knew we wouldn't – and the next morning, I sat on the lawn, looking down at Knossington Grange, and tried to imagine the future.

I still had nightmares almost every night – about the

nuns and being at Nazareth House, as well as about the things Johnson had done to me – and I had no reason to feel anything except resentment when I thought about my time at Knossington Grange. Johnson had got away with abusing not just me, but many of the boys in his care, and the fact that no one seemed to think it mattered gave a clear message that we didn't matter either. Despite that, however, I was afraid of leaving school and of stepping out into the unknown – better the devil you know than the devil you don't, as the saying goes.

An hour later, I was standing in the reception area of the hostel in Nottingham, clutching a suitcase half full of all my worldly possessions and trying – with only a very limited amount of success – to look tough and indifferent and not like a kid who wanted to go home, if only he had a home to go to.

There were fourteen other lads staying at the hostel, and I could see some of them sizing me up, trying to decide whether or not I was going to be a threat. Luckily, though, there were a couple of boys there whom I'd known at Wollaton House, and it wasn't long before I'd settled in, made some good friends and felt that perhaps things were going to get better after all.

I started work at the picture framers, and although it soon became clear that I'd just been hired to clear out their cluttered storerooms and sweep the floors, I worked hard for a few weeks. Then, when the place was spotlessly clean and well organised, I went to see the manager to ask when they were going to start teaching me the trade.

'There's not much point,' he told me. 'It's just a six-month placement. There'll be no work for you at the end of that time. We can't offer you an apprenticeship.'

So I opened the door of his office, walked out of the building and never went back.

I didn't say a word to anyone about what had happened, but I was angry and disappointed, because I wasn't prepared to spend the rest of my life sweeping floors and I was fed up with always being treated like a nobody.

Although I never really paid much attention in any of my classes at school, and I can't entirely blame anyone else for my poor academic record, I do believe that I wasn't the only boy who lived *down* to our teachers' low expectations of us. And even if I'd had more exam certificates to prove I wasn't stupid, I'm sure people would have jumped to the same conclusions about my intelligence when they heard me stuttering and stammering. It was incredibly frustrating, because I did sometimes have things to say that were worth listening to, as well as an ability to learn and to do something with my life that was worthwhile – if only someone had given me a chance.

When the manager of the hostel found out that I'd left the picture framers, he called me into his office and lectured me about my responsibilities and about the importance of not being a quitter. We argued back and forth for a while, but when he finally listened to what I was saying, he agreed with me. Being right didn't get me a job, however, and for the next few weeks I hung around the hostel every day, killing time.

I hadn't seen much of my brother and sisters since I'd started at Knossington Grange, but I met up with them one day when my mother paid one of her rare and irregular visits to Nottingham. We all met her at the train station in the morning and somehow, by late afternoon, she'd invited me to move to London to live with her, and we were back at the station buying me a one-way ticket so that I could start a new life with my mother, who wanted to make up for all the lost years.

My sisters were against the idea as soon as my mother suggested it, but they were all married or with partners by that time, whereas I had nothing – and therefore nothing to lose. When I asked them to give me a good reason to stay, they couldn't think of one. So I told myself they were just jealous because I was going to be the one to form a relationship and a bond with our mother – which was something none of us had ever been given the opportunity to do before.

I couldn't believe that finally, after sixteen years, I was going to live with a member of my family. On the train to London, I imagined being able to say to people, 'Yeah, well, my mum thinks . . .' and I had to keep reminding myself not to grin like an idiot.

The flat my mother lived in with her boyfriend, Frank, was much shabbier than I'd imagined it would be. However, anything that might have been lacking in her surroundings was more than made up for by Frank himself. I liked him immediately, and it was clear he worshipped the ground my mother walked on.

When I arrived in London, I was bursting with energy and optimism. I couldn't wait to get started on my new life and the first thing I did was sign up for a good amateur football team – which as well as giving me something to do, also helped me to make some friends – and then I looked for a job. Unfortunately, though, England was in the midst of a recession, which meant that few employers were taking on new staff, and those that were weren't on the lookout for unqualified, apparently under-educated sixteen-year-olds who'd never worked before. So I spent my time playing football and running, and tried to make do with the £1 a day allowance my mother gave me to buy a drink and a bag of chips while I was out.

I was so starved of affection and I wanted so badly to 'belong' to someone that I'd allowed myself to hope that I'd be able to build an idyllic relationship with my mother. But when she wasn't at work, she was out partying somewhere, so I rarely saw her, and when I did, I wasn't sure I actually liked her. She didn't show any signs of being crazy about me either.

Although feeding me and buying me the occasional item of new clothing didn't seem much of an expense, considering I'd cost her nothing for sixteen years, I could see she resented it and it irritated her. So, after eight months, I accepted the fact that I'd made a mistake and went back to Nottingham. I'd known the risk I was taking by going to London, but at least I'd tried, and I wouldn't have to spend the rest of my life wondering, 'What if . . .?'

What I hadn't taken into account, however, was that, in my absence, the care order that had made me the responsibility of the local authority had been cancelled and the hostel no longer had any obligation to house me. Luckily, though, they let me stay for a few nights until they could find me a bed in homeless accommodation.

I was seventeen and living in a large, filthy, rundown house, sharing a room with five men who, like all the other occupants, had long ago given up pretending they didn't drink and that they gave a shit about anything. It felt as though I'd reached the end of the road before I'd even had a chance to take more than a couple of steps along it.

Who knows, maybe all those men felt like I did. Maybe,

like me, their indifferent, tough attitude was just the façade they'd created for themselves in an attempt to cover up their total lack of hope and deep sense of loss. And maybe they felt, as I did, as though they'd been picked up by someone who didn't really want to touch them and carried at arm's length to the nearest dumping ground for people who are never going to amount to anything and aren't even worth bothering about. What I expressed was my anger, but what I was really feeling was hopelessness and an almost palpable longing for someone to care about me.

I was frightened too, because I could see my own future in the empty, bloodshot eyes of the men in that house. If they'd ever had any hope, they'd lost it long ago. None of them was going to make old bones, and no one was going to cry for them when the booze and/or years of sleeping rough killed them.

They were all old – or at least they looked old – and I was just seventeen. My life hadn't even got started, and already it seemed as though someone had tattooed the word 'no-hoper' across my forehead. It wasn't fair. I didn't want to be lumped together with all those men whose experiences had – for whatever reasons – left them unable or unwilling to face each day unless they were drunk.

I knew I had to get out of there. In the few days since I'd arrived, almost all my belongings had been stolen, so I gathered the things that remained, and left.

Of course, if you leave the place you're living in, 'homeless accommodation' becomes merely 'homeless', and for the next few weeks I slept under bridges by the river, stole food from shops or from the bins behind them, and – determined not to look like the down-and-out I'd become – washed in public toilets. I was losing weight, and as I got thinner I started to get ill. Then, one day, I looked in the mirror in a toilet in town and knew I had to find someone to help me.

'Think, Jerry,' I told myself. 'There *must* be someone. If you don't think of someone, you could be dead before you're twenty. And then you might as well have killed yourself when you were kid. At least that way you wouldn't have had to live through all the shit you've lived through.'

But there wasn't anyone. And then I remembered my brother's friend Arthur. Arthur had always been good to me and had never asked for anything in return. He wouldn't judge me or look down on me; maybe he'd give me a change of clothes, or some food.

Half an hour later, I knocked on Arthur's door, and when he opened it, I burst into tears.

It was a few seconds before he recognised me and said briskly, 'Right. What you need is a good hot bath and something to eat.' Then he took my arm and pulled me in through the door.

I stayed with Arthur for two years. He helped me get

on my feet and I found work as a bricklayer – like my father – although I couldn't always hold down a job, because sometimes I had to wait until the nightmares and flashbacks loosened their grip and I was able to function properly again. Sometimes, though, I did almost manage to believe that I was just a normal young man, leading a normal young man's life.

I will never forget what Arthur did for me, and I will never be able to repay him for it. But of all the things he did, perhaps the most important was to show me that there *are* people in the world you can trust, good people who will help you, not because there's something in it for them, but simply because you need help.

While I was staying with Arthur, I started seeing a girl I'd known at primary school. We were together for six years, and when we broke up, I spent a couple of years belatedly sowing some wild oats, although I never let anyone get too close to me, until I met Sarah.

When Sarah and I moved in together, I really thought the past was well and truly behind me. We had a baby daughter – the most beautiful baby that had ever been born – and as I held her in my arms for the first time, I couldn't stop crying. It was as though all the emotions and unshed tears that had been building up inside me for a lifetime were finally flooding out. I had virtually no experience at all of fathers, but now that *I* was one, I was going to love my child and keep her safe, and no one was ever going to cause her harm.

Maybe it was the responsibility I felt towards my daughter, or perhaps it was the memories of my own childhood that triggered an increase in the frequency and intensity of the nightmares and flashbacks that had never really left me. Whatever the reason, as they became more difficult to live with, my relationship with Sarah gradually became more distant and our arguments were more regular and pointless. Eventually, we argued about something almost every single day, and I knew that a lot of the problems we were having were my fault. It seemed as though we were hurtling towards the end of our relationship and I couldn't find the brake. I felt powerless to change anything and, in an attempt to blot out the pain and to ignore the cracks that were becoming chasms in the hope that they'd simply go away, I began to drink.

It must have been obvious to everyone except me that I was making everything worse, and when I finally reached the point at which I recognised that too, I tried to hang myself. And that's when I ended up in hospital and, a few days later, in the offices of Freeth Cartwright Solicitors.

# Chapter Thirteen

When I told my story to Mark Keeley, the solicitor, he contacted the police and they started the investigation they called 'Operation Master'. If I'd thought about it before I went to the solicitors' office that day, I'd have realised I was going to have to talk to the police – and possibly to other people as well. But it took me all my courage to tell Mark, and I would never have been able to do it if I'd allowed myself to think about what was going to happen after that.

My only real contact with the police had been when I was drunk and argumentative and had lashed out with my fists at some bloke in a pub. So although I didn't want to talk about my childhood to *anyone*, and just the thought of doing so made me feel sick with humiliation and self-loathing, policemen in general would have been very low on any list I might have made of potential confidants. But they were amazing.

During every interview I had with the police, they listened with sympathy and patience as I stuttered, mumbled and wept, and throughout the entire horrendous process that followed, they were always polite and respectful. It obviously mattered to them that justice should be done for what had happened to me and to all the other boys Johnson had abused and harmed – of whom, it soon became clear, there were many. As 'Operation Master' progressed and the police began to make their enquiries, more than twenty former pupils came forward to tell their horrific stories – pupils not only from Knossington Grange, but also from another school where Alan Johnson had worked before he went there.

It was August 1993 and I was twenty-eight years old when I tried to commit suicide and Sarah finally threw me out, and it was during October and November of the same year that I gave official statements to the police. However, it wasn't until Monday 6 March 1995 that Alan Johnson finally came to trial. I'd waited for years for the moment when he would have to face the unspeakable crimes he'd committed against the children he was supposed to be caring for and whose lives he had so irrevocably damaged – I'd waited for it and I'd dreaded it.

The self-loathing and guilt I'd felt for as long as I could remember had affected every aspect of my life, and now I was going to have to talk about what had happened to me in public, to a courtroom full of strangers. It felt as though I'd agreed to be branded with a mark that would identify me forever as being tainted and unclean.

A forensic psychologist who interviewed me so that he could make an assessment of my mental state said in his report that I was 'afraid of being regarded as irredeemably defiled' by what Johnson had done to me. And he was absolutely right. Even sixteen years after the abuse had stopped, the prospect of talking about it in court made me feel sick with anxiety. What was even worse, though, was the thought of continuing to live every day of my life with the psychological consequences of Johnson's abuse while he hid behind a mask of respectability and pretended – to himself and to everyone else – that he'd never done anything wrong. So I knew I had to overcome my dread and stand up in the witness box in the courtroom when my turn came.

Johnson was charged with twenty-seven counts of indecent assault and buggery involving eighteen different boys at two schools, and he pled 'not guilty' to every single charge.

I was called to give my evidence on the Thursday, by which time I was so sick with nerves and stuttering so badly I could sometimes barely be understood. As I walked into the courtroom, the sound of my heartbeat was pounding in my ears and it felt as though someone was wringing my stomach with their hands. I didn't want to focus on any of the faces that were turned towards me, because I didn't want them to become real, recognisable people. I looked at Johnson – just once – and although for a moment I thought I was actually going to faint, I knew I had to let him see that, despite the damage he'd done to me, I wasn't defeated.

As I stepped into the witness box to give my evidence, I quickly scanned the uniformly solemn faces of the jurors, and when I saw a woman with a sympathetic expression and kind eyes, I focused only on *her* and told *her* the answers to all the questions I was asked.

First, I was questioned by the lawyer for the prosecution, Mr Calder-Jose, and then by the defence lawyer, Mr Hunt. The judge sometimes asked me questions too, and sometimes he clarified for the jurors something I'd said that my stammer had made almost incomprehensible. And with each question I was asked, I felt my soul contracting as another part of it shrivelled up and died.

I was asked about when I'd started at Knossington Grange – how old I'd been and what I'd thought about Johnson when I first encountered him – and I said I was twelve and that he'd been like a father figure and, no, he hadn't touched me to begin with. Then I was asked the names of the other boys in my dormitory, but I was so nervous I could only remember three of them.

'And when Mr Johnson came to see you at night, what would happen?' Mr Calder-Jose asked me.

'He would come to say goodnight,' I answered. I was stammering badly and I felt embarrassed when I saw several people lean forward in their seats as they tried to work out what I was saying.

Mr Calder-Jose repeated the words I'd just said and then he nodded, as if to tell me to go on, so I added, 'And to give us a hug and a kiss.'

'Would that be a kiss on the face, or on the lips, or where?' the lawyer asked.

'That would be on the lips,' I answered, closing my eyes for a moment to try to blot out the horrible image that had come into my mind as I said the words.

The questions continued and gradually, painfully, I told the woman with the kind eyes how Johnson had started by touching me and then progressed to lifting me out of my bed and carrying me up the stairs to the art room or to his bedroom, where he'd raped me and done things to me that had stayed in my nightmares ever since.

'How often would it happen, Mr Coyne?' the lawyer asked me.

'I don't know how many times,' I said.

'Are we talking about once a month? Once a fortnight?'

'Sometimes three or four times each week,' I whispered, and the kind woman looked at me with shocked pity.

Some of the questions had to be repeated, and when I answered them, the judge turned again to the jurors to clarify what I'd said. And all the time the lawyer was pushing and pushing for the details that I wanted to tell him – because I wanted everyone to know what an evil man Johnson really was – but that had always been too terrible to admit even to myself, let alone to say out loud.

'When it was over, did he say anything?' Mr Calder-Jose asked.

'He told me that it was his secret, our secret,' I stammered.

'At the time, did you think of telling anybody about it?'

'No.'

'Why not?'

'I could not.'

'You could not? Did Mr Johnson say anything to you about what would happen or might happen if you did tell anybody else?'

I looked at the kind woman again and told her, 'He said that they would lock me away.'

'In any particular place?' Mr Calder-Jose asked.

'In a room full of spiders,' I stammered, quickly wiping away the tears that had escaped from the whole sea of tears that were pricking my eyes.

The lawyer waited while I drank some water from

the glass beside me before asking, 'Why did he say spiders?'

'I'm scared stiff of spiders,' I answered, and my hands shook as I replaced the empty glass.

'Did there come a time when you did tell somebody?' he asked, and when I answered, 'Yes,' he asked me what had made me change my mind, so I told him the truth: 'I just couldn't handle it anymore. I couldn't handle all the nightmares and I wanted to die.'

When Mr Hunt cross-examined me, he tried to discredit me as a witness and to shoot holes in everything I'd said. I hated him for it, although I knew what he was doing and I'd known it was going to happen. But when you're telling the truth, there's nothing anyone can do to 'trip you up'.

Having established the fact that I'd sometimes been aggressive and difficult to manage when I was at school and that I'd seen an educational psychologist and speech therapists, Mr Hunt asked why I'd 'never said a word to any of them about Mr Johnson and about what you *said* happened'. And then, speaking slowly and clearly – for dramatic effect and/or because he thought he was talking to a fool – he said, 'I have to suggest to you that you have made this up, Mr Coyne. I have to suggest to you that there was no interference with you of any kind.'

'Why?' I wanted to shout at him. 'Why in God's name

would anyone willingly and deliberately put them themselves through this painful, humiliating, soul-destroying process for any reason other than to right a terrible wrong and bring to justice a man who did unspeakable harm to dozens of children?' But all I said was, 'No. It did happen.'

Some years after I'd left school, I'd applied for a job at Knossington Grange and Mr Hunt raised the fact in his cross-examination, suggesting that someone who had been so badly abused would never want to return to the 'scene of the crime'.

The judge referred again to the same point at the end of my testimony when he asked me, 'Why did you want to go back to the school as staff?'

And this time I looked directly at him as I answered, 'Because I'd spent all my life in institutions and I was scared on the outside.'

The judge's voice was stern but the expression in his eyes wasn't unsympathetic as he said, 'Just tell the jury this: why did you not tell anybody about it until you did?'

'I don't know,' I answered. 'It's . . . It's just not something you can turn to anybody with.'

He nodded and said, 'Yes, thank you very much. You are free to go.' And I walked down the steps of the witness box and out of the courtroom.

It was over – at least, that part of it was. I'd never wanted anyone to know that I'd been the victim of repeated sexual abuse when I was a child. That's why I'd bottled up the shame and guilt inside me for so long. And now the whole world would know. But I had no choice; whatever the price I'd have to pay for speaking out, I knew I had to do it, because if I hadn't, Johnson would have got away with what he'd done. He'd ruined many other lives apart from mine and, as far as I was concerned, Thursday 9 March 1995 was his long-overdue Judgement Day.

When I was a child, it was that man's job to protect me and look after me, instead of which he'd continued the work the nuns had already started and destroyed any chance I might have had of leading a normal, happy life.

Speaking out at the court hearing was almost like standing up in public and saying, 'I *do* matter,' and maybe by doing it I'd taken a step on the long, possibly infinite road towards self-esteem and towards dousing the flames of the fire that had raged inside me for so many years.

When I was a boy at Knossington Grange, I'd gradually begun to realise that Johnson was abusing other boys as well as me, although I hadn't really known which boys and to what extent. But when I read the transcript of the court case and all the other testimonies, I sobbed, and I hated Alan Johnson more than I'd ever done before.

His trial by jury concluded exactly a week after I'd given my evidence. When the verdicts were delivered, the courtroom was packed with people, including police from a number of forces around the country, all eager to be present in the hope of witnessing justice being done.

As each charge against Johnson was read out, the foreman of the jury gave the verdict 'guilty' and you could hear people all around the courtroom whispering triumphantly the single word 'yes!' But I just sat there silently, with tears streaming down my face. I can't explain how I felt: they were tears of relief, of pride because I'd finally stood up and been counted, and of gratitude – to my solicitor Mark Keeley, to the police, to the woman with the kind eyes and to all the other jurors, because they'd listened to and believed what we'd told them and by doing so they'd ensured that, ultimately, Johnson hadn't got away with what he'd done. The horrible secret he'd forced so many of the boys in his care to keep was finally out in the open and they didn't have to be afraid anymore – and nor did I.

Johnson was convicted on fifteen counts of indecent assault, four counts of buggery and two counts of attempted buggery. In theory, he was given eight years for each one of the counts of indecent assault and attempted buggery and twelve years for each count of buggery – which would have added up to a well-deserved 184 years in prison. But, of course, the sentences were to run concurrently and he was actually sent to prison for twelve years.

It wasn't enough – in my eyes and I know in the eyes of many other people too – not least because the appalling harm he'd done to so many lives could never be put right. All I'd really wanted, though, was for him to be found guilty, and as he was led away to start serving his sentence, I walked out of the courtroom feeling – for the first time in my life – like a free man.

Maybe there *are* some secrets that it's okay to ask someone else to keep. But for more than half my life I'd kept a secret so terrible it had contaminated me and almost consumed me. And now that it wasn't a secret anymore, I no longer had to carry on my shoulders the crushing weight of shame and guilt that had haunted me since I was twelve years old.

Inevitably, adjusting to living without that burden and trying to create a new life for myself now that I was free wasn't as easy as it might sound, and for the next five years I drifted from one job and one relationship to another.

After Johnson's trial, I was given counselling for a few months by an amazing man called Paul Britton, a forensic psychologist who'd assessed me before the hearing, at the request of the police, and who is still one of the top people in the field of assessing and treating the victims of abuse. He seemed to know instinctively what was going on in my head and as well as encouraging me to acknowledge and confront my fears, he was instrumental in setting me on the road to recovery by helping me to understand and try to come to terms with the guilt and self-loathing that coloured every aspect of my life.

In Paul Britton's report, he wrote that he believed I had simply been an extroverted and lively little boy and that it had been the nuns' treatment of me that had led to the antisocial behaviour which later resulted in my being sent to Knossington Grange. He stated that, in his opinion, the damage that had been done to me at Nazareth House could have been counteracted and extinguished by a subsequent nurturing environment and by the care I would have received at Knossington Grange had it not been for the actions of my housemaster, Alan Johnson.

Paul Britton assessed me as being a man of 'good intelligence and a high level of compassion', and stated that my suicide attempt had been an 'intelligent response' to the emotional deficit resulting from sexual abuse, which, he said, gets to the core of a person's self-esteem and is far more difficult to recover from than the physical abuse I received at the hands of the nuns. He pronounced me 'unable to sustain employment appropriate to his level of intellectual functioning', which may have accounted for the fact that I spent the next few years working in various jobs as a bricklayer and drifting from one relationship to another – some of them good and some of them not so good.

In another psychological report, it was stated that I was suffering from chronic post-traumatic stress disorder, was at significant risk of suicide and will never recover from the effects of sexual abuse. And, certainly, Johnson's conviction and imprisonment didn't have the magical effect I'd hoped they would have.

On the day when I'd watched him pack his car before driving away from the school for the last time, I'd told him that, one day, he'd have to pay for what he'd done. At the time, the words were just an empty threat made by an angry, damaged child. But, when they finally came true, I'd hoped my psychological and emotional wounds would start to heal. And I did gain some satisfaction from knowing that Johnson had been made to face up to what he'd done. In reality, though, the harsh brutality of the treatment I'd received from the age of three years old, first from the nuns and then from Johnson, had inflicted wounds that were far too deep and far too severe to be cured instantly – or perhaps ever.

I knew I was facing a long and very difficult road towards recovery and that it was a destination I might never actually reach. What was probably the most depressing, daunting aspect of what lay ahead for me, however, was the fact that I was going to have to travel that road alone.

And then I met Elena.

I saw her for the first time coming out of a shop in the centre of Nottingham. She was with another girl, although I have no memory at all of what her friend looked like. They were talking excitedly to each other, and just at the moment when I realised I was standing completely still staring at her, they both laughed, and when she turned her head I knew she'd noticed me.

She smiled and, stupidly – because I could feel myself blushing – I looked away, and when I looked back, she'd disappeared. For a moment, I continued to stand there, feeling almost as though I'd lost something, and for the rest of the day I kept seeing her face in my mind. But there was nothing I could do, except, perhaps, go back the next day and hang around outside the shop I'd seen her coming out of, in case she reappeared, or – more likely – until I was arrested for loitering with intent.

Then, two days later, as I pushed open the door of a bar in town, she turned round and looked at me, at first quizzically, then with an expression of recognition in her eyes.

We spent the rest of that evening talking, and although I had never felt so at ease with anyone before and the thumping of my heart only told me what I already knew, there was – perhaps inevitably – a problem. Elena had been in England for just a few days, doing an intensive language course, and she was returning home to Russia the following morning.

By the end of the evening, I felt as though I'd known her all my life. Clearly, though, we were never going to be able to have a 'proper' relationship, and although we exchanged phone numbers and email addresses and promised we'd stay in touch, I don't think I dared to hope she'd contact me when she got home. So I was over the moon when, a couple of days later, she answered my email.

During the next few months, we were in constant contact – first by email and then by phone – and it wasn't long before I felt as though I could tell Elena anything, even the bad things I'd done that I was ashamed of and that I'd never talked about to anyone before. But although we may have felt emotionally close, the truth was that we were 1500 miles apart, and I began to wonder if what existed between us could really be called a relationship at all and, if so, where it was heading.

One evening, after Elena had sent me a video of her making coffee in her flat near Moscow, we were talking on the phone when I asked her, jokingly, when she was going to make a cup for me, and she answered immediately, 'When you come to see me.'

It was all the encouragement I needed.

It took two months to get a visa, and as soon as it came through, I booked a flight to Moscow.

I'd just lifted my suitcase off the baggage carousel at Moscow Airport when the nerves really hit me. My return

Jerry Coyne

flight wasn't for two weeks, so if Elena decided I wasn't as nice in the flesh as the person she'd been talking to on the phone for the last few months, I wasn't sure what I was going to do. It was confusing, too, being surrounded by people babbling away nineteen to the dozen in a language I couldn't understand. Being out of my depth, with no control over what was happening to me or around me, always made me nervous – which was just what I needed as I walked past the customs and immigration officers and waited for them to call me out of line for sweating and looking suspiciously over-anxious.

Surprisingly, though, they seemed barely to glance at me, and as the doors to the arrivals lounge slid open, I began to scan the sea of smiling faces, searching for Elena.

I saw the sign before I saw her. She was holding a piece of cardboard high above her head, on which was written one word: Jerry. She burst into tears when I put my arms around her and kissed her cheek, and for a few minutes we just stood there, holding each other close, oblivious to the swirling movement of people around us.

When I eventually pulled away so that I could look at her, I asked her about the sign.

'I thought you might not recognise me,' she told me. 'You might have remembered me as being different.'

'You're right,' I said, and the tears had sprung to her eyes again before I added, 'I didn't remember how beautiful you really are. You're perfect. You look like a porcelain doll.'

She buried her face against my shoulder and whispered, 'Jerry, my Jerry,' and I smiled as I told her, 'I *am* your Jerry.'

It's a cliché, I know, but the next two weeks really did seem to go by in a flash. We spent almost every minute of every day together, holding hands, talking and confirming what I hadn't dared allow myself to believe – that Elena was my soul mate. The day before I was due to fly back to England, I asked her to marry me and, with tears of happiness pouring down my cheeks, I put an engagement ring on her finger.

Before I stepped up to the desk to hand over my passport for checking at Moscow Airport, I turned around one last time to look at Elena, and she raised her hand as though she wanted to reach out and touch me. Seeing her tears made it even more difficult for me to leave her, and as I sat, alone and lonely, on the plane back to England, my mind was so full of her I couldn't think about anything else.

Back in Nottingham, I didn't seem to be able to concentrate on anything. I was barely aware of what I was doing at work, and in the evenings the house felt soulless and empty. I couldn't sleep, but what was worse than anything else was that, for almost two months, I couldn't contact Elena.

When I turned on my computer one morning, the screen was blank and nothing anyone did would bring it back to life. I lost everything that had been on it, including all my email addresses, and within twenty-four hours I lost my mobile phone too. I didn't have Elena's postal address and I hadn't made a note of her phone number, so I had no way of contacting her. I didn't know what to do, and for a while I almost believed that it was fate's way of telling me to forget her, so I did nothing. I found out later that she'd called my mobile every day, and when, by some miracle, my phone turned up a few weeks later and I dialled her number, she was crying so much that, at first, I couldn't understand what she was saying.

'I thought you had left me,' she sobbed. 'I thought you didn't want me anymore.'

And I cried too as I told her I would never leave her, and that nothing would ever be able to keep us apart.

'I'm coming back to Russia to get you,' I said. 'Whatever happens, I won't leave again without you.'

I flew back to Moscow at Christmas and stayed in a hotel with Elena and her parents, while I tried to work out what to do next. The temperature was an almost constant minus forty degrees, and there was probably more ice and snow on a single street in the city than I'd seen during all the winters of my life before then.

After Christmas, I went with Elena to the British

Embassy, where I was told there would be very little chance of being able to obtain a visa for her.

'Well, you're going to get to know my face pretty well,' I told the smartly suited young man who was looking at me with a serious 'official' expression but whose eyes seemed almost kind. 'I'll be here every morning for the next six months or for however long it takes to get Elena a visa.'

He must have realised that I meant it – perhaps he knew himself what it feels like to be in love and he took pity on me – because, after being interviewed for an hour, Elena was told that she *would* be given a visa and she would be allowed to return with me to England.

Even though we held each other's hand tightly throughout the four-hour flight to London, I kept turning to look at her, to reassure myself that it wasn't all just a dream and she really was sitting beside me.

Before I met Elena, I'd almost given up hope that anyone would ever really love me or want to share a life with me. I'd tried to come to terms with the prospect of always being alone, and although I hadn't allowed myself to think about it consciously, I'd been afraid that things might change between us when we started to live a 'normal' life together in England. But I should have had more faith.

Six months after I'd brought Elena home with me, we were married. She looked even more beautiful than ever in her wedding dress, and as she stood beside me in the registry office, I could hardly believe what was happening was real and not part of a wonderful dream.

Six years later, we're very happy together and I feel as though I'm the luckiest man in the world. I still have nightmares and flashbacks and I've finally had to accept that they'll probably always be part of my life. But they're much less frequent than they used to be, and when I wake up from them, I just reach out my hand to touch Elena and I know that I'm safe and I don't have to be afraid anymore.

I was just a little boy when, night after night, the nuns told me they were trying to beat the Devil out of me. I believed them when they said I was his child, and it was because of that belief and because I wanted someone to love me that I was so vulnerable to Johnson's horrific abuse. It was many years before I understood the truth – that if the Devil does exist, he can't be cast out by bitterness, anger and brutality.

I *do* have a mark on me, but it isn't the mark of the Devil: it's a wound on my soul that will never completely heal, and it's the reason that, although I don't believe in the Devil, I *do* believe in evil.

Some of the harm that was done to me when I was child – that still affects me today and will do so forever – was casually selfish and unthinking: my parents abandoning me, for example, and my teachers at primary school not wondering why I sometimes behaved badly and was aggressive. But some of it was the result of the deliberate acts of evil people – some of the nuns at Nazareth House and Alan Johnson, my housemaster at Knossington Grange. I can't forgive them for what they did to me, and I hope that, if there *is* a God, He won't forgive them either.

As I lie in bed at night, I no longer have to cross my arms over my chest and try to stay awake so that I can pray to God to protect me, because sleeping peacefully at my side is the angel who has filled my heart and driven the Devil out.